D0325732

TELLING TRUTHS
IN CHURCH

TELLING TRUTHS IN CHURCH

SCANDAL, FLESH, AND CHRISTIAN SPEECH

MARK D. JORDAN

Beacon Press

Boston

Beacon Press
25 Beacon Street
Boston, Massachusetts 02108-2892
www.beacon.org

Beacon Press books
are published under the auspices of
the Unitarian Universalist Association of Congregations.

© 2003 by Mark D. Jordan

All rights reserved

Printed in the United States of America

06 05 04 03   8 7 6 5 4 3 2 1

Excerpt from "Letter to Walt Whitman" from *Source* by Mark Doty,
copyright © 2001 by Mark Doty. Reprinted by permission of
HarperCollins Publishers Inc.

This book is printed on acid-free paper that meets the
uncoated paper ANSI/NISO specifications for permanence
as revised in 1992.

Text design by Christopher Kuntze
Composition by Wilsted & Taylor Publishing Services

Library of Congress Cataloging-in-Publication Data
Jordan, Mark D.
    Telling truths in church : scandal, flesh, and Christian
speech / Mark D. Jordan.
        p.   cm.
Includes bibliographical references and index.
    ISBN 0-8070-1054-5 (alk. paper)
    1. Homosexuality—Religious aspects—Catholic Church.
I. Title.
BX1795.H66 J67 2003
261.8′35766′08822—dc21

                                              2002151004

CONTENTS

TELLING ✝RUTHS IN A "CHURCH CRISIS"

CHAPTER ONE

W HAT YOU ARE READING began as a series of lectures delivered in Boston a few months into the "Catholic pedophile crisis." The crisis (to stay with that cliché for a moment) was provoked when the *Boston Globe* reported how the local archdiocese handled priests accused of pedophilia. The topic for my lectures had been set about a year earlier. It brought together questions I had been writing on for a decade. I had no idea that the topic would coincide with such painful months in the history of Boston's Roman Catholic churches—indeed, of the Catholic Church in America. Still, when the *Globe* stories began streaming out in early January 2002, I decided to leave the lectures exactly as they were originally conceived. I was convinced that Catholics were obliged especially in those months not only to speak about what had happened, but to try to say how things might be done differently. We were obliged to think precisely about which kinds of truth needed telling and how best they could be told into a "crisis," if they could be told at all.

Even under that conviction, delivering the lectures was not easy. Many in the audience were angry and heartsick from the shock of the daily revelations. What would tomorrow's

I

newscasts bring? Would the priest of their parish or a child-hood pastor be the next one exposed? Was the archbishop staying or going? Where was the pope in all of the turmoil? There were darker fears as well. Some people saw the grow-ing press coverage as the latest round of anti-Catholic poli-tics, the *Globe*'s revenge on not only Cardinal Law but the city's Irish establishment. Others worried that the crisis re-vealed the perilous vulnerability of churches to press attack. Others still were overwhelmed just by the suffering—of the boys or young men who had been sexually abused; of their parents and families; of parishioners whose lifelong con-fidence in their church was bitterly contradicted; of priests who had not committed abuse and were in danger of unjust suspicion; even of the priests who had committed abuse, but who were still human souls in need of forgiveness.

I was and was not an outsider in Boston. I didn't know the archdiocese, but I did know the story. In July 1997, I had watched on local television as a Dallas jury made history. Its members assessed $119.6 million in damages against the Catholic diocese of Dallas for "gross negligence" in failing to discipline a pedophile priest. The judgment set a record for cases of clerical abuse and so earned stories in *USA Today* and the *New York Times*. There was even a passing mention by Dan Rather. Like so many Catholics living in Dallas, I had been caught up in the case for weeks.

The jury's finding came in a civil trial of eleven cases in-volving Fr. Rudy Kos.[1] The cases accused Kos of having sex with a number of boys from 1981 through 1992 when they were between nine and sixteen years old. Ten of the plaintiffs identified themselves as victims of Kos's abuse. The eleventh case was filed by parents of a young man who killed himself in 1992 at the age of twenty-two. In testimony, the young men still alive described various sexual acts that Kos performed on them hundreds of times. (One of the macabre sidelights of the trial was watching the staid local newspaper trying to hint, say, at the mechanics of foot fetishism.) Lawyers for the plaintiffs then showed that the Catholic diocese had been warned of Kos's activities with boys at least as early as 1985. The Catholic diocese finally sent Rudy Kos for treatment in 1992, but while misleading parishioners about the real reason for his absence. The diocese continued to support Kos for another two years, not least by paying off $25,000 in credit card debt.

The issue in the Dallas civil trial was not whether Fr. Rudy Kos had forced sex on the boys. The question was whether the diocese was liable for allowing him to continue doing so. The jury agreed unanimously that the diocese was liable for between 85 and 50 percent of the real and punitive damages in each of the cases. Although the Catholic bishop of Dallas professed deep sorrow over what happened and eventually ordered special prayers and fasts, he wouldn't, of course, admit that he or any other official had been negligent. Some priests were bolder in defense of clerical privilege. The head of diocesan fund-raising, later removed, suggested that pastors should begin transferring assets to get them beyond reach of a settlement. A former chancellor of the diocese, who failed to act on numerous complaints against Kos, and who was almost cited for contempt of court during the trial, told the *Dallas Morning News* that the victims' parents were really the ones to blame: "It doesn't appear they were very concerned about their kids."

I watched the verdict live on a local broadcast that scorched July afternoon. There was a fat file of news clippings beside me and tablets full of notes. I had no financial stake in the outcome, but I was caught up in it. I had once taught at a local Catholic university and its affiliated seminary. In my first year there, I taught Rudy Kos.

Kos was enrolled in a remedial course designed to cram

seminarians with whatever minimum of "Scholastic philosophy" church officials then demanded of future priests. Kos explained that he was taking the course under duress. Eight years older than me, he was struggling to change over from nursing to the dusk-lit labyrinths of Latin theology. His struggles were typical of too many "late vocations"—men who entered inflexible seminaries after starting careers elsewhere. And not only careers. Kos had already been convicted of sexual abuse as a juvenile. The diocese claimed not to have known about it. It did know that Kos got a brief marriage annulled, since the diocese itself managed the annulment procedure. The ex-wife later swore that she had reported that Kos had "a problem with boys." The diocese denied.

So, what was new in the "Boston scandal"? There was nothing new in the cases themselves or the archdiocesan response to them. The pattern of abuse and cover-up was queasily familiar. What made Boston different was the extent and persistence of the national press coverage. The Kos case had flickered across the national media, but it remained essentially a local story. The cases in Boston and the responses to them became and stayed national news. Because national coverage lasted so long, the American hierarchy and the Vatican itself were finally compelled to respond. Then both the coverage and the cardinals began shifting the questions toward priestly sexuality in general. Suddenly, there was a huge and serious audience for talk about the number of gay priests in the church and what it might mean. Before the "Boston scandal" began, Catholic bishops didn't often talk in public about homosexuals in the priesthood. When pushed, they might admit that there were a few of "them"—perhaps "2 percent," certainly fewer per capita than in the general population. By the time the American cardinals were meeting in Rome about pedophilia, the president of the American bishops' conference found himself admitting that it was "an on-going struggle" to ensure that the priesthood "is not domi-nated by homosexual men."[2] *Newsweek* devoted several pages of its cover story to "the gay dilemma."[3] The coverage shifted for a while from particular cases and responses to institutional distortions. What was new about Boston was that the story was suddenly not just about Boston. It became for some time a scandal about the system of seminary formation and priestly discipline, of official speeches and their anxious silences.

The persistence of national press coverage was not all to the good, of course. Much of it was sensationalism. It re-hearsed unwittingly the old satirical complaints according to which all priests are gay and (therefore?) sexually voracious. Other publicized debates showed the ignorance of church history that is the bane of the mass media—and of contem-porary Catholicism. Splashy graphics on magazine covers or websites asked whether the church could survive, as if the Ro-man church hadn't ensured its survival in the face of much more threatening "crises." On the other side, well-groomed defenders of clerical bureaucracy could somehow still assert that the church had always fully cooperated with local au-thorities. As if the churches hadn't resisted over centuries any interference of secular authority with priestly disci-pline—and as if the Vatican weren't still claiming preemptive jurisdiction of cases involving priestly sexual relations with minors.[4]

The persistent news coverage reactivated powerful hate speeches inside and outside the Catholic Church. Church officials rolled out familiar accusations against homosexuals not only to legitimize a purge of "out" gay men from the priesthood, but to divert attention from aching institutional failures. Some outside the church got to rehearse the old stereotypes of Catholicism as a cult of idols run by demonic deviants. Everyone got to hear homosexuals repeatedly confused with pedophiles, "molesters," and "perverts."

I had my own small role in the coverage, both before and after delivering the lectures in Boston. Sitting in TV studios waiting for a "discussion" or being filmed for a momentary clip on the evening news, I kept wondering how anyone could speak truth into this cacophony. I was grateful to the news coverage for bringing forbidden questions into discussion. I was horrified at what the coverage was doing to our languages for speaking about priestly abuse, its real causes, and its practicable remedies. Before we could get any further, we would have to think more critically and more creatively about how to speak the truths we all professed to want "on the record."

I began by remembering the most easily forgotten thing: truth telling is not simple. It is not like the Norman Rockwell painting in which a ruggedly handsome white man, whose plaid collar is literally blue, speaks to the town meeting at his white clapboard church, while other white men, wearing ties, listen in admiration.[5] Truth telling isn't like that. Truth's speakers don't often radiate handsome honesty. They are disconcerting and diverse rather than comfortably familiar. They are rarely received with admiring attention. And what they have to say can seem beyond hearing—or bearing.

Then I remembered something equally obvious: there are different kinds of truth, and each requires its own ways of speaking and listening. Leaving aside the more spectacular rhetorical flights in the scripted point–counterpoint of the national press, I tried to list the kinds of truths being offered around this scandal.

It had begun with truths in files, the truth of documents and legal proceedings. Complaints were filed against a priest, and investigations followed. Settlements were arranged, and then the priest was transferred. These are the sorts of actions documents record, but only in a shorthand punctuated by silences. Some documents are saved, others not. Some letters are full and frank, but other letters are carefully plotted after long conversations that don't survive in the files. Legal pleadings, depositions, and verdicts are the products of staged recital and negotiated "facts." Documents are traces of events, but they are also elements in an official story. No matter how many revelations they seem to make, documents in personnel files or court records also record decisions not to reveal, to stick by the agreed story.

The "Boston scandal" began as well from the memories of abused children and adolescents. News reports tried to capture the content of these memories and to show something of the pathos in them. We have heard the desolate stories told on screens by trembling faces. The truth in them is at once so compelling and so elusive, so urgent and so reticent, that it cannot be captured by tape. The memories are traumatic memories, and trauma chops itself into memory by chopping up memories. I don't discount the testimonies of abuse as untrue. They are probably the truest words we have heard in the scandal. Still, their truth is not a truth of numbered propositions. It is the truth of an unclosed wound.

The scandal turned then toward the truths of institutions, of the regulations, customs, and fictions that enable the Roman church to operate. It has been hard to hold this kind of truth in view for more than a few instants, because so much of the reporting has wanted to hurry past it to policy proposals or predictions of outcomes. Institutional truths are more complicated than single policies or brash predictions, but they are also more important. Complicated and important— how do we begin to describe them? Do we need ethnographers and anthropologists to narrate for us how the cultures of the Catholic priesthood are lived out? Should we turn instead to institutional sociologists or legal historians or cultural critics? If the most hidden truths in the scandal are truths about clerical institutions, what is the expertise that could even begin to tell them?

The expertise used to be called "theology." Since the institution in question is not just any human complex but rather a Christian church, and since Christians profess that their churches are not merely human complexes, Christian theology ought to have something to say about how to tell truths in a crisis that now reaches into the core structures of the institution. Yet, theology has been notably absent in the scandal. Some people classified as theologians, including myself, have been invited to speak—in the short snippets required by our media. I'm not sure that what we have spoken is theology. To say that more personally: although I think that I managed to say a few true things about Catholic institutions in the course of dozens of interviews and not a few op-ed pieces, I don't think that I ever managed to move my words into the realm of theology.[6]

I understand by *theology* taking mature responsibility for the indispensable forms of Christian speaking. This shouldn't mean that theologians usurp responsibility for what others have to say, either by appropriating it or censoring it. The theologian is asked to take responsibility for her or his own speaking in those forms. Responsibility has to be taken in the presence of scriptures and traditions, face to face with the ablest speaking partners, before the challenge of holiness, with a special trust (badly translated as "faith"). It also has to be taken through the indispensable forms. At its best, theology is not divorced from the rest of Christian speech. It is not like a superlanguage that judges every other language. Theology is more like a new grip on language, a more supple and more deliberate handling of it. The theologian takes new responsibility for speaking in the confidence that Christian speech has already been used for proclaiming a revelation, for performing sacraments, and for efficacious prayer. Language has been sanctified. We ought to be able to use it to tell sanctifying truths—which is not the same as telling "the whole truth and nothing but the truth." Taking responsibility for speech requires being especially responsible for its inevitable failures.

Sitting on newsroom sets or waiting while reporters typed in what they heard of my hasty responses to rushed questions, I remembered finally that I should have expected special difficulties when trying to speak a few words of theology into a scandal about sex in the priesthood. Sex has always been a nervous preoccupation for Christian speaking. It has provoked some of the angriest theological words, as it has excited some of the most violent theological passions. At the same time, and not coincidentally, sex has seemed to threaten the authority of Christian speaking. Trying to speak truth about a churchly sex scandal—or trying to speak the truth about sex in church—or trying to speak what churches might be after some honesty about what sex is ... these efforts lead us right to the most awkward tasks of the speech called theology.

In the brief chapters following, you will read some parts of the original lectures I delivered in Boston. Mostly, you will find my third or fourth attempt to deliver them better. While rewriting, I have kept the conviviality and casualness of the spoken word.[7] You will hear the places where the pressure of the "Boston scandal" pushed on the lecturer and the audience. Most of all, I hope that you can catch an effort to find a way of speaking theology into institutional "crisis." In part, this will mean figuring out how to talk when so much talking has been distorted by the powerful motives of institutions in conflict. For the most part, it will mean searching for ways to enliven the oldest speeches Christians have.

TELLING SECRE✝S
SCANDAL AND CHURCH REFORM

L ET ME START, as some medieval sermons do, with a division of the theme announced in my title: "Telling Secrets: Scandal and Church Reform."

First, there is the topic of telling truths in and about the churches. Here, I explore how churches produce silence around sexual secrets that disrupt churchly power. Examples come from my own tradition, which is Roman Catholic, because those are the examples I know best.[1] I trust that you'll be able to draw analogies with your own church experience easily enough. The Roman church is old and arrogant; it is weighed down by institutional sins; it has invested in sprawling systems for keeping secrets. Still, it is not uniquely sinful. Things would be tidier if we could deposit all ecclesiastical sins into one church and then lock its front doors. Tidier, and satisfyingly self-righteous, but not truthful. If the Catholic Church has venerable ways of silencing disruptive truths about itself, those ways are answered by other systems of silence in other churches. Christian churches ought to be communities sanctified in the truth; they have often been communities in which some important truth about church was the daily casualty.

Secrets—the second part of my title and theme. Telling secrets about things that are most emphatically called secrets.

Secrets about the unnamable sin—to recall that misreading of Ephesians 5:3.[2] Secrets about that place buried in ashes, the city scorched off the plain—Sodom itself. Christian theological traditions give us not only the name or rather misnaming of these sins—or the moralizing misreading of that terrifying story in Genesis. The traditions give us the diagnosis of the secret sin of Sodom as a churchly sin, a sin frequently found in churches, a sin *of* the churches.[3] Precisely that truth cannot be told in church, and so church experience must itself be silenced.

Finally, the last topic of the title, church reform. I describe not only the ways by which churches keep silence about these sins, but also what happens or doesn't happen when the sins are finally spoken. There are relations between truth telling and changes in the regimes of silence within the churches, but the relations are perhaps not so straightforward, not so comforting as we would like. Telling scandalous secrets in the churches and the prospect for reform means telling truths about same-sex acts and desires within the churches, out of churchly experience, against well-rehearsed devices for enforcing silence, in tense hope of some change for the better.

Let me add a disclaimer. I am a gay Catholic, but I'm not interested in painting myself as a glorious martyr. We lesbian and gay Christians have our stories of suffering at the hands of the churches. It can be consoling to tell those stories and important to learn from them. The stories of gay Catholics have particular interest for me—and not just because my own story fits among them. These stories lead us right into neglected questions about church lying. But I am not about to tell my story or to recite any of the others I've heard, no matter how moving. I want instead to read beyond them to what they show about telling secrets in the Roman church.

By reading beyond the stories, I'm not suggesting that we

can neglect the dependence of "true" words on the lives of those who speak them. Christianity inherited from some ancient schools of philosophy the moral imperative of living out truth, of attending always to how you show the truth and not only to how you intone it. For Foucault, indeed, Christianity as distinct from some ancient philosophy imposes an obligation to bear witness against oneself.[4] It is a religion in which the self is constructed and managed by confession of faith, but also of sin. Gay Catholics would agree emphatically. But I add: Christian religion imposes a further obligation to bear witness against ourselves in the plural, in our efforts to live as a church. The church is (or ought to be) ours. Bearing witness against it is not an assault on an enemy so much as a testimony within a household. But the analogy can mislead. The church is ours only in view of a higher truth under which it must also constantly be corrected and rebuked. If the church is a new family, a grander household, it is still not the company of saints in heaven. So, we are obliged to live out the telling of our individual stories, and then we are obliged to attempt to tell the church secrets that begin to appear through them.[5]

With that division of the title and that disclaimer, I turn to the body of my medieval sermon, to its *dilatatio* and its *exempla*, to its analyses and its cases, on the way to an exhortation.

Patterns for Telling Secrets

CONSIDER THE SHAPES of speech that we use when we try to break official silence about same-sex desires within the Roman church. Our speech often begins by stammering, by acknowledging that we don't yet know how many kinds of secrets there are or what the most significant might be. There are secrets in or behind the official teachings, but also secrets about official people. Most of all, there seem to be secrets about the church as a sprawling set of rules, rituals, and institutions. How can we begin to talk about the institutional paradox of a church that is at once so homoerotic and so homophobic, that solicits same-sex desire, depends on it, but also denounces it and punishes it? Here, *we* means not just Catholic theologians or openly gay men who continue to identify as Catholic despite heartbreak. *We* is anyone who cares about the oldest means in Western Christianity for constructing and regulating sexual identities. The means lie now near the core of Roman power, that is, in the normatively male-on-male relations within the clergy.

Women are still sufficiently disenfranchised in the Roman church to make lesbianism a separate concern in analyses of official silence. Women's religious communities have been protected places for living out both lesbian desire and Catholic women's gifts for ministry, which are shamefully denied ordination. Of course, truth telling in women's communities has also had its own chances, its hopes and risks. Some communities, under certain leadership, can be as oppressive as any male community—and perhaps more so, because there is always a level of masculine authority above the women's leadership, no matter how autonomous that is made to seem. Official Catholic silence is pronounced by clerical men and then enforced most melodramatically by them. For that reason, gay men are solicited differently by Roman power than lesbian women are. The running subtext of Catholic clerical power is *male* homoeroticism. Perhaps that is why "out" gay men in the Catholic church often seem more timid than out lesbians—as if the men were still more muzzled or more complicit in their own muzzling. For all these reasons, I concentrate here on muzzled men, with whom I have shared too much.

What kinds of speech can we use to tell some truth about those men? Let me consider four kinds: *counterargument, testimony, fragmentary history,* and *provocative analogy.*

The first form for truth telling is *counterargument,* the attempt to reply by critique and better reasoning to official teaching, canon law, or scriptural exegesis. Much lesbian and gay theology has been written in the past thirty years as counterargument with striking results. We are much better informed now than in 1970 about how flimsy crucial scriptural translations or interpretations actually are. We know much more about the contradictory history of the condemnations of same-sex desire by Christian leaders, lawyers, bureaucrats, and court theologians. We can read with much clearer eyes the new documents that continue to rehearse bad interpretations or ignorant history, not to speak of false psychology and sociology. We see, in short, that too much Christian speech about same-sex love was and is both fallacy and slander.

Having admired much in these three decades of books, and gotten more from them than I could hope to give back, I have still concluded that counterargument is not the most helpful shape for truth telling. Indeed, it is often self-defeating. For example, it is wiser not to argue, much less to try to demonstrate, that official Catholic documents are often wrong when they talk about what they now call "homosexuality." Many of the documents don't invite counterargument because they really don't invite discussion. They are efforts to forestall discussion. We reply better to such arguments not with counterargument but with media analysis, with rhetorical reading. I generalize the example in this way: many official documents about same-sex desire are scripts for preventing serious speech by scrambling it. To avoid the scrambling, we need to expose the rhetorical devices in the documents. We should avoid endless counterargument, in

which it is possible to waste decades without getting a hearing, and choose instead a kind of rhetorical exposure.[6] Turn
from what is said to how it is said, to the rhetorical and institutional arrangements for endlessly rehearsing the same old
speeches. Making this turn, we acknowledge that the more
important secrets are not in official pronouncements, but in
official church lives.

So, I turn to a second shape for truth telling, the form of
testimony. You know the solemnities and the jokes that now
attend "coming out," the ritual origin of gay life. You know
as well that it is not a single act so much as an ongoing performance, since the normative presumption of heterosexuality confronts gay men daily. The performance of "coming
out" must vary with the setting, especially church settings.
Sometimes a gay man finds himself having to stand up to say
something like this: "I am Christian. I belong to this church.
And I now call myself 'gay' because of how I desire." The
power of those ritual words of testimony—if only there were
more courage in the churches for speaking them and hearing
them.

I don't want to feign naïveté or succumb entirely to senti-
ment. There are complications in testimony. When we tell
coming out stories, we are not giving raw experience, however raw the telling feels. We fit our stories into increasingly
well defined genres, into cultural patterns for storytelling. If
we want to rely on individual testimonies in truth telling, we
should of course admit that they are edited by understand-
able motives and by inherited narrative patterns. So is every
act of human speech. We need to be sophisticated when we
cite individual testimony, but that doesn't mean that we give
it up altogether. Not only is it required for personal sancti-
fication, it is one of the best ways of learning about the larger
patterns of male-male desire in the church. The Roman

church's knowledge about male homosexuality is to be found elsewhere than in its official documents. If you want to know what the Catholic Church understands about gay life, don't read the new *Catechism* or recent decrees from the Congregation of the Doctrine of the Faith. Look instead at institutional arrangements and practices as they are revealed by testimony. Look especially at the testimony of or about the lives of men who live closest to the exercise of institutional power, who live at the center of the institutions.

The move through testimony to institutional arrangement and practices brings us to the third shape for truth telling against the official silence, the genre of *fragmentary history*. Archives hold testimonies from the past. The archives are disordered, incomplete, contradictory, but they offer many memoirs—including memoirs of clerical sodomites. The memoirs are written mostly by hostile observers, but they can be nuanced by comparing them with the much rarer accounts "from inside." These memoirs can then be enriched by looking to reforming tracts or jeremiads, to anticlerical polemic, to love poetry and iconography. After all, the sodomitic priest is hardly something new in Europe or America. Nor is he alone. Other figures of churchly sodomites appear in the archives: the lecherous school-brother, the naïve and feverish novice, the senior hermit grown overconfident and sloppy in his daily austerity. Together, the archival traces of these figures give us what we can call a history, that is, a composite account of the "life" of a community, a religious congregation, or a clerical arrangement.

I call this history "fragmentary" to remind how disorderly and incomplete it is. We will never have anything like a satisfying history of same-sex desire in the churches, in part because evidence has been systematically suppressed—or never registered. The history will always be scattered and ambiguous. But that doesn't mean that it has no value. There is an extensive churchly "science" of male homoeroticism, a long institutional experimentation with it, especially in monastic communities or federations, in later religious congregations, and so in a normatively celibate clergy modeled after them.

The fourth and final shape for trying to speak beyond official silence draws *provocative analogies* between Catholic clerical culture and what we now see in explicitly gay subcultures. We can picture clerical gayness more clearly because we have detailed analogies to guide us. For the first time in much more than a millennium, public and well-developed homoerotic cultures exist in the West *outside* the Christian churches. We are particularly familiar with how contemporary American men build gay networks or neighborhoods. So, when we come to the distorted and fragmentary evidence of American clerical gayness, we bring clearer pictures for comparison. When we turn back to homoerotic cultures inside the Christian churches, we now know what to look for.

In some of my work, I have compared features of seminary formation to efforts by urban gay enclaves to ritualize coming out or to pass down cultural practices without reproductive families. I drew attention to the denied desire in seminary formation that encourages sexual abuse. Again, I explored the clichéd comparison between Catholic liturgy and drag in order to understand that fabulous creature, the Liturgy Queen.[7] These analogies have proved provocative. A reviewer in *Publishers Weekly*, for example, found one discussion of liturgical drag "more like a *Saturday Night Live* skit than a serious effort to reshape Catholic discussions about sexuality."[8] To which I was tempted say, there's more truth in the monologues of "Father Guido Sarducci" than in many approved surveys of priests and seminarians.[9] Satire is a common form for telling truths about priests because some of those truths can only appear as satire. Indeed, it would be a good thing for theologians to relearn the art of satire, which is very different from the invective that they often use in describing each other's work. Take truth wherever you find it, but also speak the truth in the ways it must be spoken. Satire may be the only way to speak secrets against overwhelming efforts to hide them. Again, the homoeroticism of official Catholic life is sometimes so blatant that only powerful devices could keep us from laughing out loud at its solemn denials. My deliberately provocative analogies were offered as helps to releasing our laughter—so that we could begin to tell what we already know, but cannot yet say.

The analogies also shift the burden of proof by troubling the heterosexual fiction of official talk. Instead of pretending that every Catholic priest is *of course* heterosexual underneath his celibacy, why not consider the alternative? Why not consider that some, many, most of the American priests now on active service might have a homosexual orientation by one or another criterion? Once you allow this consideration, innumerable points of analogy with other gay communities leap forward. Now the burden of proof is to show why we shouldn't take those resemblances seriously. Is it because every Catholic priest is *of course* heterosexual?

So far, I've offered four shapes for trying to tell Sodom's secrets in the churches: counterargument, testimony, fragmentary history, provocative analogy. Let me turn now to the kinds of reactions these forms often provoke.

Reactions to the Genres of Truth Telling

O FFICIAL CATHOLIC reactions to disclosure of these sodomitic truths are much more varied in my experience than the shapes for trying to tell them. The speed and variety of the reactions must baffle any effort to survey them. Otherwise, they couldn't hide what they are supposed to hide. So, instead of attempting a survey, I talk instead about three more general reactions that share a rhetorical device: they try to silence truth telling by broadcasting the kind of scandal that sounds so harshly around us right now. The three reactions broadcast scandal by pretending to make claims: that the truth telling is *angry*, that it is *anti-Catholic prejudice*, and that it has *no proof*.

The first reaction is to claim that any effort at telling these secrets is *angry*. The reaction looks like a moral judgment, but fails to make clear any moral rule or guide. Is the rule that we should never be angry—"gentle Jesus, meek and mild"? That rule is hard to sustain from Christian Scriptures and traditions of moral theology. I hear in them rather that we can be angry—that we must be angry—when trying to tell some truths about violence, about the oppression of the powerless, about the cruelty of greed. Or does the reaction suppose instead only a rule against directing anger at Christian churches? The implicit rule would have to be something like this: when you try to tell a truth about the churches, you may never do so angrily.

I might accept such a rule as a piece of strategy. We are sometimes likely to achieve more if we speak calmly than if we shout. Sometimes. I can even understand the rule as a caution against unkind anger within Christian community. Life together in churches is trying. As Romano Guardini says, the defects of the church are the cross on which Jesus is crucified—and so the cross that a believer must accept to follow Jesus.[10] Trials of churchly living shouldn't be an easy excuse for rupturing community by unkind irritability. Still, that hardly implies that we should never be angry at our churches. Remember Beverly Harrison's magnificent title phrase, "The Power of Anger in the Work of Love."[11] We might say—as Harrison does—the *necessity* of anger in the work of churchly love.

How to distinguish the anger of love from the anger of hatred? What sets corrective anger apart from annihilating anger, the passion to remedy from the passion to destroy? There can be no general rules in answer to such questions. The only "rules" for discerning among angers will look like paradoxical cautions or challenges. I have seen Christian anger that is both truly loving and hot. I hope that I have sometimes felt it. But the Roman church squanders human energy in efforts to deny that there can be any such anger directed against itself. Any dissent is labeled as unjustifiably angry, because only irrational and inappropriate anger could lead a Catholic to dissent from Roman authority. Catholic women who ask for their place at the altar *must be* hysterical. Lesbian and gay Catholics who criticize their churches for doctrine or practice *must be* consumed by bitterness—and surely by self-loathing as well. Of course, the real scandal is not in women or in lesbian and gay believers. The real scandal is found (in two ways!) in an institution that tries to defend itself by projecting a field of distortion onto its members.

Projected scandal distorts the motives for dissent or criticism. The motives are reduced or falsified. What gets dismissed as "angry" criticism is often speech that comes after long sadness, out of old suffering. Or it is speech that demonstrates enduring care for the churches. Wayne Koestenbaum writes, "Anger (among its many uses) is a form of flirtation."[12] We might add, "angry" dissent is a way to woo one's church. It is not jealousy or hurt feelings so much as deep disappointment at the way churches deform themselves. The anger that can correct a church is like the anger you feel at lovers who destroy themselves by giving in to their worst impulses. You are angry with them because you love them and cannot sit still while they work their own destruction.

Loving anger is not only for the sake of the church, of course. It can also be for yourself. It is a means of survival within the churches, of staying on without being crushed. In this and many other ways, anger can be exercised as a form of Christian fidelity. Every official reaction that dismisses dissent as "angry" must distort this motive most of all. By definition, then, dissent cannot be loving or faithful. It must be the opposite of loving and faithful—it must be egotistical or hateful, lapsed or rationally depraved. Official reactions cast scandal on the motive of Christian anger in order to rule its words out of hearing.

If the label "angry" doesn't accomplish its work, other general reactions stand at the ready. There is a second claim or accusation, the charge of *anti-Catholic prejudice*. Consider this potent charge as a means for enforcing silence about disconcerting truths. The charge begins by declaring that the uncomfortable speech falls below the level of rationality. It is mere prejudice. The charge then declares that the speech comes from an outsider—worse, from a traitor. You must remember what treason means in a clergy that still nurtures memories of persecution by a fantasized Protestant ascendancy or a feared Jewish plutocracy. American Catholics are still encouraged to think of themselves as the perpetual second-class, whose colleges are not the "best colleges" and whose taste is always suspect. Someone who speaks against the church has gone over or, rather, "up" to the social victors, the perennial enemy. No need, then, to listen to what the person might be saying. In fact, there is a tribal obligation not to listen—to stuff up your ears so that you don't hear.

Notions of churchly loyalty and betrayal are closely linked

to fantasies of Catholicism as tribe. For some "old Catholics," the tribe is marked out by shared experiences of growing up in settled parishes, with novenas and grade schools—parishes that once had Catholic bowling leagues and that still do have the Knights of Columbus and guided tours of the Holy See. The boundary around this Catholicism is a set of memories in which family life, school, and parish cult are intertwined. "The church" is one of the forming circumstances of one's growing up—maybe the matrix that held together the parts of growing up. To speak against it in dissent is to violate family and heritage, the identifying past. The tribal boundary can reach further to articulate itself as official theology: obedience to the church's official structures is the defining moment of Catholic identity. By either reasoning, to be Catholic is not to criticize in public too loudly or at all. To criticize is to betray—and so to disqualify oneself from speaking.

To label a speech as mere anger or as treacherous prejudice rules that speech out of hearing. A subtler and sometimes more effective way is to repeat a demand that it *produce proof*—the third general reaction. Every time an effort at truth telling starts up, the reaction says, more and more loudly, "Prove it!" The tentative truth telling starts up again. It lays out analyses, weighs their persuasiveness, charts their complexities. "Prove it!" The reaction is an interruption. It forestalls speech by demanding what it will never specify. After all, what would count as proof? Nothing, it turns out, because every class of evidence has been discounted in advance.

I agree with many others that contemporary reports of same-sex desire or activity in high church offices are easily sensationalized or misinterpreted. The sexual activities of bishops or popes are reported to us only through the language of scandal. That was the case in 1970 when the publicity-hungry French writer Roger Peyrefitte began to hint

that Archbishop Montini loved a Milanese actor before being elected Pope Paul VI.[13] Scandal! Of course! Look behind
the cry "Scandal!" which only says more explicitly what
"Prove it!" implies. Look behind it to see how it reduces stubborn truth telling to silence.

Let us assume just for a moment that there was convincing evidence that the man who became Paul VI once had a
male lover—please hear me: this is a momentary assumption.
Let us assume that we had depositions, photographs, financial records, and other circumstantial evidence of the sort
that would make a passable case at civil law. What would be
the official church's first response to that evidence? Would it
be to weigh the evidence candidly and fairly? Or would it be
to insist that the evidence must have been fabricated—because it is inconceivable that a pope once kept a male lover?
And what if the evidence kept mounting? I suspect that the
next official response would be something like this: "We are
as shocked as anyone. The church is filled with sinners, and
sometimes even those in important church offices fall short.
Of course, theirs is a personal failure. It says nothing about
holy church. The exaggerated and still dubious evidence of
personal sin—on which we cannot decently comment—is
being used to smear the whole church." Both the hypothetical evidence and the imagined official reaction would say
painfully much about a clerical system that protects its secrets
by projecting scandal onto legitimate efforts to tell them.

I use this hypothetical case as an *exemplum*, a preacher's example, to make a point that would be much more painful to
make from the real cases unfolding around us. In the cases
around us, we are not dealing just with personal sin. We are
dealing with the sin of a system for keeping secrets—about
which we can no longer plausibly claim to be shocked. In that
system, every sin of sexual power is multiplied by the sins

of silence needed to conceal it. These sins include repeated demands for evidence that will never be acknowledged or examined.

Three more general reactions to truth telling: labeling the telling as angry, denouncing it as antichurch prejudice, demanding that it produce evidence when all evidence has been ruled out in advance. The three reactions cooperate to generate silence around disruptive secrets. They generate silence by posting scandal at the border of what gets to count as true. Tales about male-male sex in the church are officially declared untruth by being declared scandalous. The projection of scandal as a border around church secrets marks off a field of silence in which words behave strangely—even when they are used in approved church speech about same-sex desire—in thundering condemnation or contemptuous denigration or tight-lipped offers of cure. Sodomites—sorry, they are now to be called homosexuals—homosexuals are to be denounced or mocked or called to treatment—but not too often, because you mustn't give the laity ideas. Even Catholics who count same-sex acts or desires as sinful must see that this system reduces pastoral outreach itself to a strained silence, because frank condemnation or honest correction would bring the words for those acts and desires too close to the structures of churchly power. The reactions against truth telling prohibit any detailed speech, even the speech of detailed condemnation. The cost of keeping some secrets is a multiple betrayal of the Gospel. It is a betrayal not just of Gospel precepts, but of the Gospel command to preach good news. Keeping certain sorts of secrets about the institutions is a systematic denial not only of facts, but of our responsibility for the church's actions and arrangements. Keeping secrets in these ways contradicts most seriously the command that we exert ourselves to preach the Gospel as truth and in truth. Not one of us is ever free from entangling lies about our own lives. Does that mean that we should spend our energy on systems of untruth to house our ordained preachers?

Telling Reforming Truths

WHEN I LOOK BACK on my own flawed efforts to tell secrets in the churches, I detect various motives. First, I wanted to console individuals, including myself. Gay Catholics, and especially gay Catholic priests, religious, and seminarians, get trapped in repetitive suffering. Perhaps it would help them to hear out loud, in public, some words about the endless dialectic of homoeroticism and homophobia in Catholic hierarchies. I do get letters or phone calls from people who say that they have been helped. Listening to them, I am quite certain that their discoveries are their own, that my texts were only an occasion or (at very best) a stimulus to their self-understanding. In the same way, speaking or writing was an occasion for me to "work through," in the psychoanalytic sense, some of the intense ambivalence I feel toward the Catholic Church on questions of same-sex desire. The church gave me the material for building a first homoerotic identity, anxiously secret, at the price of obedient complicity in the church's public denunciations of my loves.

Were my efforts to console or to move beyond complicity a contribution to church reform? Yes, of course, so far as changes in individual Christians are the only elements out of which any larger reform can be compounded. But also, no, of course not, because I didn't put forward a plan for a new and better church. I didn't mean to. Since I think that argument is plainly not enough to counteract the field of silence, I hoped at most to show its character—to force it some ways into plainer speech. I proposed for the future only the search for a form of community in which lesbian, gay, bisexual, and transgender (LGBT) Catholics could discover how to speak their lives in faith more fully.

Any program to reform the church's secrecy about homosexuality in itself or in the world can become just another form of complicity. Catholic teaching on same-sex desire is connected to fundamental questions about clerical culture and church power, about the church as a community under the Spirit, about the church as an instrument in our redemption. Teaching on homosexuality cannot be reformed without raising those questions—not to mention questions about human sexuality as such, the theology of gender, the category of body, the nature of moral law, and so on. There can be no reform just of the teaching on homosexuality. Any attempted reform of the teaching that doesn't deal with those other matters is a sop—an invitation to be complicit yet again with an improved program of silence. The same is true for any national policy for pedophilia that doesn't address the crime's causes in institutional silence. That kind of policy is not a solution so much as an evasion. It reaffirms the basic complicities, which it is obscene to call loyalties.

When medieval sodomites were caught by inquisitors or civil authorities, they were coerced to confess according to fixed protocols. A sodomite is supposed to say certain things about his (or more rarely her) unnatural acts, filthy desires, and unbounded treacheries. A sodomite is scripted to be a certain sort of sinner. In the moment of condemnation, perhaps especially in the moment of condemnation, the sodomite still has a churchly role to play. So, too, do "homosexual heretics" under the present regime of church power. If you are going to be a heretic, be a good heretic. Fulfill the scripts for heresy—be as arrogant and stubborn as Farinata in Dante's hell, or be deformed by lechery, or be addled by superstition.[14] You will be rewarded, in a curious way, for your final performance. You can hope at least to be registered in church records as a properly punished heretic. If you are something grander, the leader of a sect, a grand heresiarch, you can hope to have your false teachings violently excerpted and anathematized for later generations of seminarians. Homosexual heretics are solicited, then, to play a final role within the churches: a role of approved denial, of denial that can be contained once again by the field of silence.

We homosexual heretics must refuse this last role—and much more the role of scapegoats for pedophilia scandals. We must not let ourselves be confined to simple genres of heresy telling, to the approved speaking roles for treacherous dissent. I take this to mean that we cannot tell our truths only within the approved genres of theological disagreement, genres devised to contain dissent. Nor can we stop with speaking our truths as criticisms against particular teachings or practices. We need to tell our truths against untruth, but we need then to tell our truths against half-truths, premature truths. We need liturgical prayers and hymns, novels and poems, hagiographies and histories, moral tracts and systematic theologies in which same-sex love appears as what it is and ought more plainly to have been: life under grace. I apply this imperative even when LGBT theologies are counted in as special voices, as boutique voices, within more tolerant churches. We will be trapped once again if we allow LGBT theology to be an add-on, a hasty supplement to the "real" speech of the churches. We accomplish full speech when we can speak fluently in any genre of theology or spirituality or liturgy or homiletics—and then beyond them, into new or refashioned genres.

We must then confess how poor our fluent speech will be

and how confining our new genres. I have sometimes felt in the last months that the most honest lecture on telling secrets in the Roman church would begin as a whimper, then rise through fevered moans, racing syllables, hoarse shouts to end in a high scream—unbearable, unmeasured, unrelieved, the scream of centuries of believers deceived, abused, tortured, executed by the church in defense of its "purity," that is, its power.

Then I remembered some lines from Simone Weil on what she calls the "cry" of the "afflicted" (as we are used to translating *malheureux*). "Even for those in whom the power to cry is intact, this cry almost never comes to express itself, inwardly or outwardly, in coherent words. Most often, the words that try to translate it ring entirely false."[15] Again: "Affliction is in itself inarticulate. The afflicted silently beseech to be given words for expressing themselves. There are epochs in which they are answered. There are others in which they are furnished words, but badly chosen ones, because those who choose them are strangers to the affliction they interpret."[16]

Our efforts to tell truths about a church for that church cannot end with the contented conviction that we have spoken it all—and very well. Our efforts at telling truths about a church cannot be accomplished by proposing or implementing church reforms—however important those reforms are. Let us do those reforms, then let us remember the cry that lies beyond them, the cry that beseeches us for words.

Preaching Violent Silence

S OME DAYS, some centuries, the cry of the afflicted was preceded by another sound, the voice of Christian preaching. Preaching came first, because it was in not a few cases the announcement of new affliction. That is one reason that this chapter has evoked, perhaps too obviously, the structure of some medieval sermons.

Grander and more influential than its modern Catholic counterpart, the medieval sermon accomplished reforms. It inaugurated crusades and announced new patterns of apostolic life. It condemned the sale of church offices and demanded mandatory celibacy. The medieval sermon was also the means for popularizing the emerging moral theology, with its violent condemnations of the newly elaborated figure of the sodomite. Preaching on sodomy could produce immediate and violent effects. Some sermons ended with hunts for sodomites, who, once caught, would be beaten and imprisoned or else quickly burned. On other occasions, cities responded to preaching by adopting severe criminal sanctions against sodomy. Even when the consequence of preaching was neither so immediate nor so obvious, medieval sermons encouraged the many kinds of delayed violence that we now associate with hate speech.

We should recall the venom in sermons on sodomy—or, now, homosexuality—for at least two reasons. First, the sermons, medieval and modern, show us how a "theology" can twine with real or threatened violence to produce silence around affliction. Then, second, the sermons may shock us into reflecting on how dreadfully shapes of Christian proclamation can be misused in order to mangle truth. My single example is from Saint Bernardino of Siena, the extraordinary preacher and church reformer from the fifteenth century. I choose precisely one of his less colorful texts, a Latin "sermon" that was not meant to be preached, that served only as a kind of compendium for topics useful in preaching.[17] I choose it because it is neither directly violent nor particularly vivid. When Bernardino preached in the vernacular, he could turn his listeners into a mob, enticing them with the imagined smell of burning bodies. But even at his most official, at his calmest, he "preaches" what produces a violent silence around the topic of male-male desire. In this respect, my medieval example proves curiously contemporary.

Bernardino's *On the Horrible Sin Against Nature* takes the form of a Scholastic sermon; that is, a highly schematic development of nested scriptural texts. Each of the sermon's three articles has its own scriptural *thema*, and the threefold division of the whole derives from the first verse of Psalm 13: "They are corrupt and they have become abominable, and in their pursuits there is no one who does good, no, not one."[18] This verse refers to the triple horror of the sodomites' crime: its corruption, its abomination, and its reprobation. Bernardino dilates at greatest length on the first of these topics, which allows him to speak of the horrible corruptions of sodomitic society, of the kinds of communities sodomites form in order to spread their insidious message and to recruit.

Bernardino blames parents for permitting their sons to have "bad connections or associations." He excoriates them for giving sinful example and for encouraging sons in effeminacy. Alas, the production of Sodomites or "Gomorrans" is not confined to the home. The very next section of Bernardino's treatise describes the many ways in which the "homeland" can become a "womb" for bearing Sodomites. In some places and times, cities have erected a dreadful "gymnasium," a "palaestra" in which the most beautiful "ephebes" could learn and practice sodomy. Even without a dedicated building, sodomites shape their own geography. Still, the place of sodomy is not so much a building of brick or stone as a building of words. Its corruption is suffered especially in speech, in the triply false speech by which "Gomorrans" seduce young men. They flatter in order to ignite desire, then they bribe with false promises of money, clothing, entertainments, and much else. Finally, they overwhelm them with "corrupt and degrading words"—words describing sexual acts, perhaps, or words of self-justification. Things have come to such a pass, Bernardino exclaims later, that whole books are written promoting sodomy and attacking holy matrimony!

All of these points for preaching are indexed to the Christian Scriptures. Bernardino connects his description of a widely diffused sodomitic system with the scriptural texts on the destruction of Sodom. The dangers to a beautiful boy growing up in Tuscany are reinforced by extended quotation from Genesis 19:4–17. The clamor rising from the Tuscan countryside is the same clamor that drew God down to the cities of the plain. The very voice of the Gospel, which is just now the voice of Bernardino, beseeches the sodomites as the angels beseeched Lot: get up and flee from your homeland—which has become a city given over to this vice, to these people. Every society of sodomites is to be understood as a colony of Sodom, and the full force of scriptural condemnation is to be brought against it.

Bernardino does not mince words. He is even willing to speak candidly about sodomy as an affliction of some clerics. In this sermon-treatise, he considers the case of the preacher who is "infected with this sin." When preaching in the vernacular, he goes further to admit that there are sodomitic theologians and prelates.[19] The admission is meant to be scandalous. Indeed, Bernardino's whole preaching surrounds the subject with scandal. He preaches against those monstrous others, those infected foreigners, who are poisoning Tuscany and polluting the church itself. Scandal silences more disruptive truths, both about who the sodomite really isn't and about what church institutions really are.

Bernardino's sermon-treatise is almost 600 years old—

and still very familiar. In America, contemporary Catholic preaching against homosexuality doesn't lead to immediate executions or imprisonments, however much it tries to influence government policy against equal civil rights. We are still told from Catholic pulpits that Genesis and other biblical texts condemn homosexuality as an intrinsically objective disorder. We hear that homosexuals are responsible for pedophilia or other sexual abuse in the clergy, as they are responsible for corrupting seminaries. Colonies of Sodom have been secretly planted inside the church. They must be uprooted! The preaching is always about *those* sodomites or homosexuals, never *we* sodomites or homosexuals. The corrupting influence is always represented as foreign, never homegrown. So, the scandalous preaching of reform misses both what really needs reforming and how much affliction preaching itself produces, even when it seems to turn away from violence.

Much contemporary preaching shares with this particular treatise from Bernardino what I call the violence of the official voice. Bernardino has incited mobs to hunt down sodomites and has inspired city governments to authorize their execution. But in this treatise, he is the voice of the Gospel of John, beseeching them to turn away, to come home. So, too, with contemporary sermons that are not evidently offensive, that are "pastoral," that "reach out" to poor homosexuals in their misery. We know just what that reach is worth in a crisis like the present one. We are always the bishops' children, never more than when we can be blamed for their failures.

As the original form of Christian proclamation, sermons ought to tell life-giving truths. They have often been the speech in which disconcerting truths are censored, elided, silenced. We need to retrieve the sermon as a form of truth telling. We need to remind ourselves that the principal obligation of the person in the pulpit is to bear witness to the truth, no matter how it upsets us. Then we must recall that preached truth must represent itself as an always-incomplete truth telling. It should represent, not fictions about polluting homosexuals, but the multiple voices of affliction. A sermon needs to bear witness to truth in an open play of voices, through a deft series of forms, to simultaneous audiences of diverse characters, each of them finally exhorted. The exhortation is to reform—which means, to repent of the scandalous silence, to learn truer speech, to practice more justice in action. But the exhortation goes beyond reform. It goes toward the cry of the afflicted—including the cry of souls whose affliction has been, *is* a menacingly silent Christian church.

TELLING L⊕VES

SAME-SEX UNIONS AND CHATTER ABOUT MARRIAGE

T HE SILENCE OF SCANDAL—produced by scandal, managed by scandal—should be resisted, but it cannot easily be overcome. Genuine calls for clerical reform quickly enough seem endless. So, too, does the effort to represent the cry of those afflicted by one of the Christian churches. Pursuing the silences produced around priestly sex requires that we look at other effects of silence around sex, and it leads us to expand any picture we might have of telling truths in church.

Throughout the last chapter, I narrated efforts of truth telling as a dialogue or rather lack of dialogue within a church, between church officials and church dissidents. Now I take up a more complicated situation. The situation involves church officials and church dissidents, but also leaders and writers from the lesbian/gay "community" (as it is called) and—what is most important—the incessant babble of our common "entertainment media" and their advertising—or rather, of our common media that *are* essentially advertising. The issue for each of these voices is church blessing of same-sex unions. The play of these voices around the issue makes up what Scholastic theologians called a disputed question. The voices in the dispute are hardly uniform: they are articulate and stammering, established and outcast, aggressively present and almost forgotten. One obligation for truth telling in a dispute is to hear all the pertinent voices before speaking any determination.

Waiting at the Church Doors

T WO WOMEN or two men come to a church door. They profess Christian faith, and they seek a Christian blessing on their life together.

The doors of most Christian churches are now locked against them. We are easily preoccupied by the doors—by strategic quarrels over keeping them closed or forcing them open. The chatter in those quarrels makes them endlessly repetitive. Before starting another round of quarrels, we would do better to freeze that approaching couple and to consider how many speeches compete to describe their arrival at church.

Consider speeches "inside" the church. Depending on which kind of church it is, there will be various layers of official talk, from doctrinal or disciplinary rulings down to the pronouncements of local bodies or the resident pastor. The layers do not agree, especially when we distinguish what they admit in public from what they profess in private. Disagreements also pull at denominational or cross-denominational academic theology. Variously accredited theologians teach for and against same-sex unions. Behind their present speeches there rise countless layers of historical texts, in which various Christian traditions have tried to describe and discipline both marriage and same-sex desire. The historical layers are supposed to inform or support present speeches. Often they are ignored, edited, or falsified, not least by the devices of managed scandal.

Consider next speeches "outside" the church. National

lesbian/gay groups have their own "official" pronouncements on same-sex marriage. They issue policy statements,
they deplore incidents of oppression, they endorse particular
reforms of church discipline. Much less organized, and much
less publicized, are lesbian/gay groups or individuals arguing
against Christian blessings. They produce "theoretical" and
political speech that resembles and partly descends from earlier critiques of bourgeois marriage by "lesbian separatists"
or "gay liberationists." If the historical layers of constructive
lesbian/gay speech are neither as thick nor as public as those
in Christian churches, they can still sometimes be heard as a
heroic or repressed past. Of course, they are also ignored, edited, and falsified.

I have yet to mention the loudest speeches about same-sex
unions between Christians—indeed, about Christian marriage simply. These speeches resound both in the churches
and outside them—though *resound* is at once too weak and
too definite. Sometimes these speeches insinuate, sometimes
they bellow, most often they are heard as the inevitable back-
ground of any conversation—like Muzak in a mall. I mean
the mechanically reproducing icon loops that chatter at us.[1]
At most Christian weddings, the chief ritual specialist is
not the pastor or priest, but the wedding planner, followed
closely by the photographer, the florist, and the caterer. More
wedding theology is supplied in fact by *Bride* magazine or *GQ*
than by any dozen academic treatises on holy matrimony.
The icon loops circulate as highly repetitive scripts for marriage and sex, scripts that prescribe words to be spoken, but
also actions to be done, looks to be copied, feelings to be
practiced, and unrealizable ends to be craved. The circulating scripts quote Christian elements, but transform them in
the moment of quotation. What is more important for us, the
mechanical icon loops thoroughly infiltrate Christian teach-

ing and worship. On "Christian" call-in radio shows or "orthodox Catholic" TV panels, in "biblical" guidebooks for happy homes or "Marriage Encounters," we are offered—we are bombarded with—barely edited versions of mass-market marriage. The more elaborate offerings combine sitcoms with pop psychology. The less elaborate are sitcoms with churchly sets.

We see the icon loops every hour, both Christianized and non-Christianized. They cannot be avoided. They jump out from the mandatory public TV screens and from glossy covers in grocery checkout lanes. It is boring even to mention how common they are—and that may be the most telling thing theologically. We forget to consider the effect on us of the bombardment of mass icons of marriage. Church leaders complain regularly about the effect of negative icons on believers—all those stories about adultery and divorce, about easy sex and no children. Indeed, one cardinal in the Vatican blamed the present Catholic crisis on the "pan-sexualism" of American society. Sex everywhere! But Christian marriage everywhere, too! Only it is not really sex—and not really Christian marriage: just their icon loops. Not Christian marriage, but ceaseless chatter in its name. When they supply these scripts or assist in their mechanical reproduction, Christian theologians reduce their own speech about marriage to chatter.[2]

The two women or two men still stand at the church doors, asking as church members for a Christian blessing. Their awkward insistence is a fateful moment both for the Christian churches and for gay subcultures. On the inside, they threaten to provoke a belated honesty about the old confusions and civic compromises hidden under the phrase "Christian marriage." On the outside, they call for a new candor about the myths of same-sex mating. Thinking through church blessings of same-sex unions allows us to dream a kind of marriage among Christians that would be less vulnerable to mass scripting, at a time when that scripting ought to be an urgent issue for Christianity. Instead of rejecting same-sex couples as the worst triumph of an alien "gay agenda," the churches ought to welcome them thankfully as a reminder, inspired from within, of how to bless Christian unions apart from marketplace law and against marketplace religion. In the same way, lesbian/gay advocates and critics of church unions ought to recognize a challenge to conceive relationships otherwise than by selling more icons of perpetual orgasmic bliss.

Two women or two men at the church doors in search of a blessing—that ought to be an invitation to make common cause against the lucrative and systematic lies that are much more damaging to Christian speech about marriage than a blessing for same-sex couples ever could be.

Chatter about Christian Marriage

L ET ME TRY TO GIVE sense to this claim by telling some plain truths on both sides of the locked church doors. I start on the inside. I start indeed from the awkward reminder that there is no "Judeo-Christian tradition" of marriage. Christian and Jewish traditions disagree about a number of fundamental issues, including the value of celibacy, the permissibility of polygyny or concubinage, and the grounds for a divorce that permits remarriage. There is also no single "Christian tradition" of marriage. Christians have disagreed with Christians about the value of celibacy and the grounds or procedures for divorce. They have disputed the role of civic authority in marriage and the spiritual value of married life. Indeed, and as you know, disagreements about the nature of marriage were at the heart of Protestant and Anglican reformations.

The quarrels are older than Protestantism. They are coded into the contradictions of early Christian texts on marriage, including canonical texts of the New Testament.[3] How could there not be contradictions? Christianity was the religion of new birth—birth into new bodies, families, and communities that were not supposed to belong to "the World," that were precisely not biological bodies and reproductive families. New Christian bodies, families, and communities wanted to reject certain obvious needs of city building. Marriage presented them all too clearly: the fallen pleasures of a perishing body, the divisive claims of blood family, the jurisdiction and even ritual superintendence of civil governments. So, of course Christianity was slow to develop its own marriage rites or codes, not to speak of a theology of marriage. The slowness spreads over centuries, not decades. After centuries, medieval Latin-speaking churches did indeed construct a theology of marriage. They also began to assert exclusive church jurisdiction over marriages between Christians through a system of church courts and hefty volumes of Latin marriage law—which much provoked Martin Luther. Any serious discussion of Christian marriage must contend with these old quarrels. Since they are quarrels about fundamentals, since they have produced enduring schism and threaten to produce more, they cannot be read as momentary misunderstandings within a unified theological, liturgical, or pastoral tradition.

Christian marriage has a past troubling enough to shock any Victorian matchmaker. The record illustrates again and again the vulnerability of theological views to programs of civic power or civic cult. Our Christian theological inheritance is a library-maze. Right alongside courageous and hu-

mane pleas for the beauty of uncoerced and affectionate marriage, there are volumes of forgotten compromises with the
procreative or property schemes of vanished states and mar-
kets. The library contains volumes that are worth a lifetime's
attention. It can take more than a lifetime to sort the volumes. In the meantime, we should remember that there has
always been both Christian speech and churchly chatter
about Christian marriages. Remembering this alerts us to
features of the current dispute about marriage in many
American churches. Consider, as one example, the appropri-
ation by churches of the current political debate about the
"decline" or "collapse" of the family. Reformers and antire-
formers alike relish statistics that show changes in American
marriages. Some of the statistics are interesting. Some of the
most interesting are the most dubious. When it comes to
"measurements" of sexual behavior or intimate attitudes, results of surveys deserve much more skepticism than they
seem to receive. They may get off so lightly not only because
our common culture confuses numbers with knowledge, but
because these numbers are so immediately useful to various
political and ideological programs, including some within
Christian churches.

Our resort to statistics about the decline of marriage is just
one sign of how we relinquish the labor of theological thinking about human life, how we give in to chatter. There are
others, including the uncritical use of political slogans as central terms in church debate. The phrase "family values" not
only displaces older Christian terms with the neologism
"value," it tacitly endorses the shrill slogan of a very particular political campaign. It also denies the many Christian
critiques of the family. Heterosexual couples who criticize
same-sex unions as unscriptural ought to remember how
roughly the canonical Jesus treats their marriages. To its early

critics and advocates alike, Christianity was a fierce challenge to "family values." If some want to argue that "gay activists" in the churches are trying to impose an agenda alien to the Gospel, they ought first to concede that any partisan boosterism for bourgeois marriage is itself a gross and palpable imposition on what canonical Scriptures show us of Jesus.

As polarized, political speech about marriage clothes itself in patches of Christian language, it strips away speech from the churches—it steals language that Christians have fashioned at one time or another to converse about marriage. Christian models of marriage are spliced into icon loops of the American Family. Far from resisting this mythology, politicized "church" networks vie with each other in popularizing it. Doing so, they make theological consideration of alternate voices more and more difficult. They gleefully hand over the few words we have left.

Chatter about Gay Mating

SO FAR, MY EFFORT has been to tell some plain truths to the chatter about marriage inside the locked doors—and the old churchly contradictions chatter conceals. Without unlocking the doors quite yet, let us pass through them—as observing angels—to listen for confusions in speeches outside, the speeches about gay mating. Let me stress here again that I am using the word *gay* in contrast with *lesbian*, and let me add a disclaimer similar to one in the last chapter. If gay and lesbian relationships are often lumped together in law and theology, not to mention political polemic, they ought to be carefully distinguished for truth telling. However gender categories behave in same-sex relations—and I come to that in a moment—they cannot be homogenized. Women who desire women were grouped with men who desire men in Romans 1, and ever since they have clung together to defend themselves from the churches. But their relationships are not the same. So, let me talk as best I can, which is from my experience of the myths some gay men hold.

It isn't hard to sketch an argument that gay couples are more vulnerable to the distortions of advertising—or ideology in advertising—than even officials in Christian churches. When gay couples come to be married, they bring an indescribably rich variety of personal motives, but they often speak these motives through a small set of stereotypes. Many of these stereotypes are reversals, inversions of icon loops of the American Family. But gay men have recently become direct targets of aggressive mass icons about their mating—that is, their purchasing.

Gay men are indeed overrun by mass representations of what their mating is supposed to be. If we were once told who we were by police officers and preachers, we are now targeted by the advertorials of glossy magazines. Gay men today are supposed to be like the stereotyped American teenage girl from the 1950s drive-in movie—and not just in having wasp waists and pushed-out chests. We are supposed to learn how to form relationships by reading advice columns and buying accessories. Some of us are like those teenage girls in another way: we are still caught in the tritest comedies of marriage and their predictable reversals. The boys breakfast at Tiffany's, then head for Fire Island and its pines. Our loves can end happily only in the wedding chapel—though they have to begin in the bathhouse (and may get back to it rather sooner than later). So, gay chatter about relationship oscillates too easily between wistful imitation and campy inversion. Some gay men speak about a marriage that differs in no respect from the suburban sitcom. Others profess to want exactly the opposite—as opposite.

Camp is parody, resistance, and critical improvisation. It is also unrequited love. The vulnerability of gay mating to icons and their inversion comes in part from a long romance with mass culture—that is, envious and disdainful collaboration in the mass culture of romance. Some of the most powerful icons of popular romance were produced by gay men and then camped by gay men. The songs of Judy Garland or Barbra Streisand, the domestic comedies of Rock Hudson, the Brady Bunch, the Broadway musical, Madonna—these are in various ways gay products, gay fetishes, and gay jokes. Their use shows how gay love camps "straight" love stories, but also adores them, consumes them. Hence, our special vulnerability to manipulations of mass culture. We are particularly sensitive to shifts, displacements, distortions in the mechanical loops of romantic reward—or its perpetual deferment.

The oscillations in the icons for gay mating should make it interesting to theology. There are ways in which the icon loops for gay love can help one resist the hypnotic narrative of romance precisely by taking it to its limits. Same-sex love tends to exhaust the possibilities in icons of romance. Consider the cliché that same-sex relationships are somehow, curiously, the distillation of romantic love. As the troubadours knew, romance is more vivid when staged against social or legal prohibitions and more captivating when kept back from any accomplished "ever after." Alison Lurie, in her bittersweet retelling of the "marriage" of James Merrill and David Jackson, records a sophisticated version of the cliché: "Their union was not celebrated in magazines and films and popular songs, approved by relatives, and legitimized by the state. No outside pressure kept them together, as it did so many of us— only the magnetic force of their own love."[4] The "magnetic force" is not only a cliché. It may well have been real for the two of them, for a time at least. It seems quite real to many male couples, holding on to each other despite oppositions. But then this sort of romance is also a potent icon loop, perhaps one of the most potent.

The icon loops are designed to construct our most intimate motives, even as we tell them to ourselves. When the loops run against each other, as competing advertisements, the results can be confusing, especially to those who are "feeling" them. Consider what happens when many gay men try to explain the motives that lead them to a Christian marriage. Listen to how that desire sometimes gets told. Certainly, many gay men say they want "acceptance" from an institution—the "family"—by which they are badly wounded. They seek full support from their families and through them by childhood or contemporary communities. They strive to fit back into a comforting social structure and to align themselves with powerful institutions that will defend their basic civic rights against encroachment.

These descriptions of what is desired in a blessing sound to me largely civic. I mean, they don't require a church. They could be secured by any sort of civil union ceremony acceptable to the families and communities. What more do *Christian* gay men say they want from a *church* blessing? When I ask this question, I often hear bits of the last paragraph again with small changes. Certainly, many gay believers say that they want in blessing the "acceptance" of an institution—the "church"—that wounds them badly. They want to be ratified as full members in it. Being married in the church is a sign of unreserved acceptance, as ordination is for those called to ministry. Gay men want support from their religious families and larger communities. They strive to align themselves with a powerful institution that ought to help secure and defend their basic rights as Christians.

These religious motives still sound to me curiously civic—as if the church were just a parallel institution to the state or nation. By contrast, I believe that Christian marriage fails to be itself when it becomes another rite of social acceptance. Church membership is not supposed to be a weak substitute for civic citizenship, and so we might want Christian marriage to be something more than a social ritual resulting in a valid license. Some gay couples certainly do want more. They want to make their relationship real by offering it up to God. Or they seek God's help in saving the relationship (according to several senses). Or they desire blessing on an existing relationship after they "convert" or "return" to the church. Such requests to be married often come with an even more urgent request for spiritual support and direction, as well as a strong claim on full engagement in word, worship, and sacrament. Churches sometimes fumble when trying to answer these requests, not just because they come from a gay couple, but because they demand something more than the deeply impoverished churchly discourse of marriage as a state function. I take this as a moment of challenge for a gay couple. It is a challenge to articulate their request as insistently as they can, precisely so that it will outlast repeated offers of chatter. Indeed, such a spiritual request by a gay couple is not so much a challenge to the churches as a gift to the churches. It may also be the most generous of motives for seeking church blessing on gay lives together.

I hesitate to say more, because I am aware how unfair I may sound. Same-sex couples have had to suffer so much from the churches that it is unfair to ask them to give back to the churches a fine gift. But that unfairness is built into Christian life, and so I will continue for a bit more. My suggestion is that male–male Christian couples have the theological gift of being caught between icon loops. There are the oscillating icons of gay chatter, which try to reconcile or at least juxtapose (formerly Christian) romantic icons (or their symmetrical inversions) with queer mockery of Christian marriage. Then there are the icon loops produced by churches intent on collaborating with the propaganda of the American Family—or else simply inverting it into its (impossible) opposite. In short, a gay couple may find itself trying to step into multiple, contradictory icons that stretch and twist each other like a row of funhouse mirrors.

Being caught between competing icon loops is a disconcerting situation and a very good one. It's not as though a couple could stand outside the bouncing icons and play them off against each other. But a couple could use the conflict of mechanical scripts to create new possibilities for combination—which is theological improvisation, creation.[5] For example, they can put the utopian icons from the earliest "gay liberation" next to icons from current chatter about gay relationship. Feminist and gay liberationist attacks on bourgeois marriage in its religious forms dissolve well-marketed ideology about marriage that obscures Christian thinking. Much pop mythology about marriage dissolves in the acid of activist critiques—and not a little church talk goes down the drain with it. And so for the bankrupt discourses of Christian marriage as the building block of This Great Nation of Ours. Why should we go to church to take a pledge of allegiance when we can do it at the courthouse?

This is the unfair challenge and the gift of gay couples caught between chattering icons: as they pass through the church doors, they ought neither to abandon their habits of camp nor their suspicion of church institutions. Going to the altar shouldn't be submission to the "mainstream." A gay union ceremony ought rather to be an epiphany of the outcast at the center of an all too established church. And the epiphany must not be televised.

From Chatter to Disputation

L ET ME NOW try the experiment of unlocking the doors. Let me see whether we can't gain something for truth telling by bringing the discourses from outside and inside together—which is to say, by letting the disputed question unroll.

The first thing that the disputation must do is to deny that there is an outside and an inside for theological thinking. The truth of any pertinent voice counts for the discussion. There is no segregation between holy and unholy voices, no sound-proof barrier around a City of Holy Speech. Those inside the churches suffer corruption of language just as much as those outside. Voices inside can fall into chatter just as easily as those outside—indeed, perhaps more easily, since the claims made by voices inside are often much higher than claims outside. Most important, both inside and outside are under the sway of mechanically reproduced icon loops. So, let the disputed question gather its voices after taking the church door off its hinges and against the inescapable accompaniment of the chatter of the icon loops. There is no escape. We can only talk over them—or rather under them.

The next thing is to ask why we need this dispute. Clearly, same-sex unions are, in this generation, right on the front line of the unending war over Christian orthodoxy. It is interesting to ask why this issue is now on the line, but it is more interesting to see how odd the present battle line is. Theologically considered, marriage is not the place to defend Christian orthodoxy or even orthopraxy. If you were going to draw liturgical or ritual battle lines, you would do better to draw them around baptism or the Eucharist. When "Christian marriage" becomes the battle cry of orthodoxy, it speaks more of the reigning icon loops than of the Gospel—or it shows how far mechanical chatter has eclipsed the Gospel.

We need to change the way the disputed question is put. We do this by noticing what all the voices suggest. In fact, the process of the dispute is not to apply a test of orthodoxy, but to take another step in hearing the truth wherever the Holy Spirit has nurtured it. A disputed question is a way of truth telling because it brings new voices, new disciplines, and better questions into theological thinking. So now with what first appears as the question about the orthodoxy or permissibility of same-sex unions. The unfamiliar voices gathered around the question may show that the question has not been asked very thoughtfully by theologians.

What can be learned from the voices gathered around about how to ask the question more cunningly? We might begin with a correction. While Christianity has anciently been marked by ambivalence toward "the city" and "the world," its doctrines and symbols are now fully spliced into the mechanical icon loops that light up American cities. This is not just a lamentable result of a few "decadent" decades. Many of the romantic monuments of the dominant civic culture, many of its canonical works on love, many of its marriage styles were once the products of a more specifically Christian artistry. Precisely for that reason Christian romance is likely to confuse itself with the circulating mythologies of marriage. By contrast, oppressed lesbian and gay cultures can still provide a reminder of how not to confuse yourself with the civic majority. However much those cultures have now been targeted by the scripts of advertising, they hold memories of what relationships are like in the catacombs. Most American Christians have no idea what it is to marry each other against the state. Many lesbian and gay Christians do.

Christian churches should bless same-sex unions not least because doing so would affirm that Christian relationships

are built against the civic icons of stable property and patri-
otic procreation. Christian churches have a charge to sanctify human relationships that is entirely distinct from the
power states delegate to them to perform legally binding
marriages. Same-sex unions give the churches a poignant occasion for fulfilling that charge apart from and even against
the state. Given what was argued in the last chapter, you will
understand that I am not advocating that churches become
counterstates with their own bureaucracies and delusions of
grandeur. We Christians have suffered too much of that. I
do advise that we should be cautious before well-practiced
systems of coercive power, including state marriage laws.
Churches should offer to bless same-sex unions for reasons
of justice, out of the impulses of Christian love, and in fidelity
to Jesus. They should also want to do so as a way of reminding themselves not to give over Christian marriage entirely
to the county clerk or the local divorce court.

Underneath the new chatter about gay mating there lie
older patterns of resistance. They offer clues to same-sex
couples for framing new speech, for conceiving alternate relations, and for enacting different sorts of "romantic" sub-
jects. They offer the same clues to any attentive theology.
One of the first suggestions by way of new language is not to
quarrel too much over the word *marriage*. If the states and the
state-like churches want the word, let them have it. I have
been content with the word *unions* because it seems to me a
more apt word for what Christian churches should be concerned with. Some same-sex couples refer to themselves
ironically as "married." Theologians might want to use the
word ironically given what the icon loops for marriage show.
Union is a much less dangerous word.[6]

Once we begin to change the question under dispute in
these ways, other changes will follow. For example, the dis-

pute over same-sex couples offers an occasion for theology to recast its traditions of thinking about sex and gender more generally. Same-sex unions can teach Christian marriage about the equality of partners and its negotiated asymmetries or reversals; about the breadth of the meaning of "procreation"; about the intrinsic created goodness of *eros*, a goodness worth fighting for. But same-sex unions can do this teaching clearly only after they have been divided by gender. In the beginning, at least, male–male unions raise different questions for theology than unions between women.

Op-ed writers and talking heads often seem preoccupied with biological or economic disparity in the "benefits" of marriage for men and women. These analyses apply to same-sex unions only after translation. The voices proposing same-sex unions would suggest that the disputation look in another direction, at the fit between approved masculine or feminine roles and expectations of the marriage union. Many jokes suggest that men are less suited for same-sex unions than women. Despite gender camping, the antipathy of masculinity to commitment carries too easily from heterosexual couples to gay couples. If gay couples were once asked, "Which one of you is the girl?" they are now asked, "How can two guys possibly stay together?" You see that this is the same gender expectation expressed two ways.

Theological thinking about gender in same-sex relationships has to get beyond the latest efforts to assimilate gay gender to normative masculinity. However "butch" they are, however many "cuts" of abdominal muscle or baseball caps they command, two men in an erotic relationship are not performing normative American masculinity. They are still performing a gender role shaped by the historically enforced distance between gay relationships and social, political, or economic acceptability. And this is a very good thing. Gay

unions have a history of subversion, fracturing, and improvised survival. They put to theology new topics for disputed
questions, such as temporary or nonbinary marriage. If
attended to, the experience of gay couples illustrates the possibility of multiple, complementary marriage rituals—of a
clear separation between civil and religious beginnings or
endings. Then they call into question what happens to masculinity when it is doubled in a relationship.

Blessed same-sex relationships have most to teach Christian theology in contesting the prevailing civic scripts for
male and female. Christian theologians have rewritten gender expectations in the past, and some do so now. Still, too
much of Christian theology about marriage simply appropri-
ates gender roles from mass culture or the civic expectations.
Christians pronounce marriage between a "man" and a
"woman." The terms are not adequately disputed. The theological assumption seems to be that the genital or reproductive distinction is clear enough and so the rest follows.
Same-sex unions require that we look precisely at the relation
between the genital or reproductive foundation and the gender edifice that is supposed to stand on it. Theology can learn
from same-sex couples how much of gender is performance:
much of what we think of as "man" can be performed by a
woman, sometimes much better.[7] So, too, with gendered
erotic expectations. These expectations prescribe not only
who gets penetrated, but who pursues, how often, and with
what delight.

Same-sex unions can show churches how to take apart
civic scripts for "man" and "woman." The scripts can then
be recombined, even to the point of having "woman" and
"woman" or "man" and "man" in an erotic partnership that
enacts most of what Christian theology has wished for good
marriages. So, one of the favored notions for Christian mar-

riage must be redone—the notion of gender complementarity. If there can be "one flesh" that is not "man" and "woman," then the foundation of marriage is not a union of cosmic opposites. Perhaps something other than gender complementarity could be used for the Christian metaphysics of marriage. "There is neither male nor female" in Christ (Galatians 3:28). Some read this as an unrealized hope for equality between the sexes. We might also read it as a call to resist doing marriage theology on the basis of an assumed gender duality.

New Terms, New Voices

AFTER GATHERING TRUTHFUL VOICES, after trying to juxtapose them in helpful ways, the convener of a disputation must mediate from voice to voice. This is best done not by privileging one of the voices, but by making a new structure of language that is able to hold some of each together. For example, in many medieval disputations, the question is "determined"—which is not the same thing as being settled forever—by proposing new terms for the confusions uncovered in the conflict of terms already in use. The same thing should happen in our disputation. The basic terms employed by all the contending voices give way in front of questioning—"same-sex" or "same gender," "male" and "female." The terms give way before voices just recognized as speaking theology.

Presenting themselves at the church door, a same-sex couple should appear as honestly what it is. This means that it necessarily appears as a sign of contradiction. We can wish that same-sex unions were not an issue in the churches, but what we live in the churches is battle over these unions. So, a couple coming to the door takes on responsibilities—of special courage and clarity about motives, but also of special care in the terms through which they speak themselves. When unions are no longer a battleground, the responsibility for special courage or clarity may disappear. The special responsibility for speaking will not—so long as being lesbian or gay is theologically significant.

This special speech has been described as testimony. Lesbian and gay testimony will be most powerful—and most important to theology—when it is the persistent refusal to be an identity. Gay couples have a special responsibility in the church to speak about themselves. They are under no obligation to confess who or what they "really" are. On the contrary, they serve the church best when they slip out from the easy confession. One gift same-sex couples give to the church is their refusal to abide by the names the churches put on them, including easy names for the love that they hope will transform them over time.

Testimony also has the advantage of reminding us which voices are excluded still from our disputed question. I am thinking of voices that discipline themselves to speak carefully about love in time. Alongside the policies of LGBT organizations, beside the liberationist critiques of bourgeois marriage, lesbian and gay writers have also been experimenting with how to write their loves. Please don't take this as a dewy-eyed endorsement of every bit of lesbian or gay fiction or poetry. Not a little of it replicates the forms and themes of heterosexual models. Not a little of it reeks. Sometimes it is the same pulp fiction, with nothing but body parts changed—and the clichés for describing them are borrowed, too. Still there are other lesbian and gay writers who try to write afresh about same-sex loves. Their efforts, their accomplishments, need to be included in our disputed question as *auctoritates*, as theological authorities.

Can the literature of love fit within a disputed question? Can it be combined with the terms of academic theology?— To which the reply is: How could we possibly exclude it?— The objection continues: But Christian moral theology is not about particulars. It is a rigorous effort to clarify the general language of moral truth.—To which the reply is: That is indeed one dominant model for moral theology. There are others. And does anyone really want to maintain that the language of most academic theology is more rigorous—more thoughtful, careful, disciplined—than the language of good poetry? Christian morals have been taught authoritatively in parables and prophecies, in the lives of saints, in visions. They are taught daily in the lives of the members of our churches. Languages for describing those lives are much likelier to be found in poetry than in scholarly essays—or so my reading would suggest.

The worst poverty in current disputes over Christian marriage may come not in assumptions about genitals or genders, but in the breezy carelessness with which theologians and pastors chatter on. Indeed, a besetting sin of Christian moral theology is this tendency to wax ineloquent about human things without any appreciation for what it takes to talk about them honestly. Before we start arguing about whether to bless same-sex unions, or the defense of marriage, or relations of procreative to unitive ends, or the sacramental bond, could we stop long enough to acknowledge how much inventiveness is required to talk seriously about human loves at all?

Theology can be adept at swallowing theories, and particular theologians have done much to incorporate theories of human love from the psychoanalytic to the behaviorist. Ingesting bits of theory is not the same as bringing a new voice into a disputed question. A voice comes not only with its own shape for speech, but with the resources to reshape itself. Before we get to the high-theoretical disputes over principles and models, we need to be sure that we have done the "low" duties of hearing or reading well. In the case of love, these duties include recognizing what love does to ignite language and to cloud it over.

Christian writers now called "mystics" know that love breaks language open. They supply vocabularies and grammars for theological reflection on love. The "determination" of our disputed question could gain much by juxtaposing their inventions with current experiments in writing lesbian and gay loves. (After all, male Christian mystics write of their marriages to Jesus.)[8] If that seems too odd or too difficult, the disputation could at least show itself sophisticated about the shapes of speeches for love. Sophistication might mean borrowing brilliant catalogues of figures in a lover's speech or recalling the consolations and the deceits of potent old stories we tell ourselves about love.[9] Sophistication would also examine the ways in which same-sex desire has already expressed itself through Christian languages of friendship or mystical union, just as "homosexual" persons have written about themselves under the guise of "heterosexual" speech. Sophistication would take the notorious difficulty of translating love poetry as a sign of how deeply embedded in particular languages love is.[10] A sophisticated theology of love would insist, above all, that the languages of love change with the time of love. There is the stammering of new love; there is the suffused terseness after years together.

From the last section of Mark Doty's "Letter to Walt Whitman":

> *And now I write from home, most of the day*
>
> *gone. Paul's done the laundry, and downstairs*
> *on the couch reads Proust. Soon we'll go out*

for Vietnamese. We have what amounts
to marriage—sexy, serviceable, pleasant,

plain. You might have lived like this
awhile with Peter Doyle, who now can say?
Of our company in your century,
Dust and silence almost all erase.[11]

"What amounts to marriage": "sexy, serviceable, pleasant, plain." Under the erasure of homophobic history, Doty imagines Walt Whitman and Peter Doyle living like that "awhile." Living out the "plainness" of a love through a while, through a domestic time.

"Sexy, serviceable, pleasant, plain." If Christians profess, as I think we should, that daily erotic love sanctifies, we should be careful not to chatter past its mystery. (If we do not profess this, then we should treat marriage either as an evil or as a matter of strict indifference to the faithful.) We should remind ourselves of the standard of serious poetry—or, if that seems too grand, of how spouses write letters over regretted distance, of the ambiguities and disclosures between long-time companions after midnight.

Bringing lesbian and gay voices in the disputed question over same-sex unions should remind theology how a community invents languages about its love. Because American "homosexuals" are inventing ways to speak against the "dust and silence," they show vividly what new love language can be. It is a privileged moment for their language. It is a moment theology should study. Theology should invite the discourses of same-sex love not only for what they say, but for how they say—because how they say may help theology remember that it ought to tremble before putting words to *eros* in time. If a Christian marriage really is a holy icon of the relationship of Christ to the church, how astonishingly difficult it must be to describe even a single Christian marriage. If we have in this holy icon the most cogent refutation of all the mechanically circulating icon loops, how carefully and cunningly we should record our experiences of it.

Mark Doty is, in the eyes of some pastors, living much less than a Christian marriage—being, as they would say, a miserable homosexual and a fallen-away Christian. But Mark Doty struggles at home in Provincetown, with his considerable talent, to tell some truth about his growing love for a man named Paul in the wake of the searing death of his last lover, a man named Wally. Mark Doty struggles in each word of these lines to say something worth hearing about the *eros* unfolding in his life. How much more ought Christian theologians and pastors to struggle in describing erotic relation as an icon of the living God? They ought to shake right through when they approach the task. They ought to, but they usually don't. Instead, too many of them begin to pronounce about who has real relationships and who doesn't, about which *eros* can be blessed and which can't, about how lifelike the latest icon loops have become.

My point is not to endorse Mark Doty's depiction of gay domesticity, although I found it more than a little attractive. I am pointing not to what he pictures, but to the care that he takes in telling truth about an erotic relationship over time and in time. Other gay writers tell truths about different relationships, including those that would be much more challenging to Christian thought. We need to hear those truths, too. Most of all, we need to watch what it is to make languages for telling how relationships unfold in time.

We stopped the couple at the door. We should have stopped our silly language about them—and about all couples. Are we now ready to enter into the disputed question about same-sex unions under the obligation to learn from

every pertinent voice, ready to be taught how frightfully su-
perficial so much moral theology is, eager only to have the
truth told—no matter what it is? If not, we should keep
silent—or at least direct our combativeness at the real corrupters of Christian marriage, who speak to us so glibly from
screens and billboards, from amplified pulpits and creeds that
splice together whatever they want to sell this week.

Until we are ready to speak again, we are not ready to begin determining this disputed question.

TELLING G⊕D
HONESTY IN THEOLOGY

CHAPTER FOUR

T HE MOST VIVID Christian languages for love are found
in what we have come to classify as "mystical" writings,
though that word is almost entirely misleading. In these texts,
we allow Christian authors to write out their loves for God
in detail, as poems and visions, as letters from various epochs
of a love. The languages of our ordinary loves, even in their
erotic heat, are applied, sometimes graphically, to the love of
God. Reflecting on the inadequacy of our languages for human loves leads quickly to mystical texts and the inadequacy
of our language for the love of God. There are other connections still.

We are following the complications of telling truths in
church. We began with devices that resist truth telling around
same-sex desire within Catholic structures of clerical power.
Together, these devices ward off serious discussion with the
shield of scandal. Scandal blocks truth telling and inures the
public to truly ugly disclosures when they do finally come.
The challenge was to find ways to tell truth against church
scandal in the hunger, not for immediate "reform," but for
more apt ways to talk about churchly abuse and its effects—on
silenced sufferers, on all those in church.

We stepped forward to the more complex situation for
truth telling in the current quarrels around same-sex unions.

59

Here, the emphasis was on the number of voices in play around the disputed question. Loud voices "inside" and "outside" the churches lead the conversation away from uncomfortable histories and unruly presents—away from the contradictions of "the Judeo-Christian tradition" or of gay mating. The loudest voices—or the most resonant—are mechanical voices of the looped scripts for marriage. We may be able to resist them, and help make a language for talking about Christian unions, by pushing theology to confront the poverty of so much of its speech about married love. What our disputes so easily lose and so urgently need is the hesitant, concrete, half-hidden language about how *eros* changes with time.

The complications of truth telling in the first two lectures point to one deeper still. This is the complication in telling *any* truth about God. We fail of truth telling in church crises or marital theology in part because we forget the original quandary of Christian speech. No human language is adequate to God's name or nature. Thus, no human language is adequate to describe human beings so far as they are images of God and sharers in divine life. Bad moral theology is encouraged by us forgetting that all theology ought to be negative theology, theology under the command to confess the failure of language. We would do better at moral theology if we weren't so miserably arrogant about our capacity for speaking truth about God.

The "Tradition" of Negative Theology

YOU HAVE HEARD THAT "negative theology" or the "negative way" or "apophatic theology" was a tradition in both eastern and western forms of Christian theology. To describe it that way is already to denigrate the tradition by reducing it to a tedious historical fact. Negative theology is not an eccentricity that flickered in and out of view in some remote place at some best-forgotten time. It is a persistent challenge to theological practice.

The challenge is comprehensive. It is not a preliminary rule in theological grammar, a sort of finger wagging to be performed at the beginning of a *magnum opus*. Ritual hand waving by systematic theologians: "While you're reading my tomes, remember every hundredth page that the best description of God may be a denial, a negation." That is not what negative theology means. Nor is it just a detour into that remote desert known—or denigrated—as mystical theology. Another kind of hand waving, waving away from a risky road: "Some strange people, unstable nuns, and wasteland monks experienced God as growing absence, as no-thing." Negative theology is neither a grammatical caution nor a fringe phenomenon. It is an event that rewrites Christian theology from scriptural exegesis through systematics to liturgy or pastoral care. It confronts the whole of Christian theology with the clear-eyed reminder that human languages cannot say who God is or what God does, even (or especially) when they are truly sanctified.

Negative theology does not confront us for the sake of being clever or obscure. It confronts us on behalf of the pastoral in the original sense of that metaphor. Negative theology hopes to prevent the limits of human language from blocking a soul's progress toward God. (Let me use the old language of "soul" for now without objection, if only because it is the language of the voices I am trying to rehearse.) Consider someone who falls in love, not with a person, but with a caricatured image of a person. So long as the lover clutches that image, refuses to give up that image, the lover can never move toward the person represented by it. Negative theology wants to rip through the image so that love can mature into love of God as God is, not as God is named by us.

Since negative theology is soul leading, it is always more process than accomplishment, more practice than perfect conclusion. Negation keeps humbling theological language at every point—to make it more inventive as an aid in caring for souls. I say "inventive" because the application of negative theology to Christian language frees it from artificial constraints, such as academic guild rules or the other exclusions we saw at work around the disputed question. When you think that a certain piece of language can capture God, you fix it and give it privileges. When you *deny* that any human language can capture God, you free Christian speech to improvise upon any helpful form or genre, any structure or style.

To begin, the tradition of negative theology draws on each shape in Scripture: it speaks as liturgical prayer and hymn, as persuasive oratory and private letter, as commentary and practical instruction. Negative theology may indeed restore our sensibility for the effect on us of the shapes of scriptural writing.—I take as a sign of dulled sensibility that we rarely feel the need to explain how the preferred form of Christian theology can be anything other than a life story told four ways.—Negative theology then reaches beyond scriptural forms to adapt any form for writing that urges the lover forward to God. Indeed, we can now recognize that our impulse to open the range of the disputed question to voices with different shapes for talking about love was the impulse of negative theology. It broke language open in anticipation of God.

Dionysian Sequence

L ET ME ILLUSTRATE this process of breaking open by noting something obvious about the writings of the theologian who is usually credited with being the source of negative theology for Western readers: "Pseudo-Dionysius," that is, the writer who around the year 500 c.e. took the pen name "Dionysius the Areopagite" from the Acts of the Apostles.[1] Through centuries we have speculated about who Ps-Dionysius really was and why that person might have chosen the pseudonym. (You may also remember that the identity of Ps-Dionysius was once a prominent topic for Protestant and Catholic dispute. How times have changed.) We don't need any of that speculation. We do need to notice something about the texts we inherit under the name Ps-Dionysius. Whatever else you want to say about them, you must first say that they are meticulously organized as a sequence. They are meant to have a certain order, a beginning and an end.[2]

When most people mention negative theology, they refer to two works in the surviving Dionysian writings; namely, the *Divine Names* and the *Mystical Theological.* The *Divine Names,* to speak much too simply, tells why no affirmative name for God is adequate, from the most physical to the most metaphysical. God is neither a rock nor being-above-being. Then, the *Mystical Theology* cancels out every possible name, affirmative or negative, in a breathless sequence of denial. These two treatises by themselves are steps in a process: a process that begins in the middle of Scriptures, then moves through other shapes for speech about God (including what the Greeks called philosophy) to culminate in a meditation on what happens to language as it draws near God. Language must be stripped away, layer by layer, beginning with the most physical names and ending with the most metaphysical, until you end your flight into God by denying even your denials.

These best-known Dionysian writings care for souls by moving from their idolatry of language into God. The movement doesn't stop with that string of negations from *Mystical Theology.* It goes on in two other works. A third book traces

God's generous love as it moves through the whole cosmic order, from the angels down, in orderly descent and ascent. A fourth book follows Christian community and liturgy as they pull us into the cosmic procession and back to God.

Why doesn't the sequence of treatises end with *Mystical Theology*? Why does that string of breathless denials fall in the middle of the Dionysian writings as we have them? Let me suggest two answers, both true. First, it is easier to sketch out a string of negations than to write with appropriate self-correction about churches. Dionysius's *Mystical Theology* writes of the highest things, but abstractly. Abstractions are safer than the necessarily more specific language about the churches, which tempts you to believe that you know exactly what you are talking about and can capture it in language without much worry. Writing rich moral or liturgical theology is more dangerous linguistically than sketching the final flight of the soul beyond speech, because moral or liturgical theology can sound literal. Most Christians will not believe that God is literally a rock, but many seem to believe that moral ordinances or counseling categories or liturgical rubrics might be literally (and perpetually) true. Literalism is a much stronger temptation further "down" in the cosmic hierarchy.

A second answer about the position of *Mystical Theology* is that its severe negations are the best preparation for concrete theology, for reflection on the churches. They not only urge us to apply negation throughout theology, they remind us that the goal of human life stands beyond human life as it appears to us—beyond the names and rules and institutions that we confect to order lives here. You can't write concrete theology appropriately before you sketch out the sequence of negations as best you can. Otherwise, you will take your language in practical theology much too confidently.

I freely admit that there are many problems in the latter books of the Dionysian writings as we have them, including a dangerous emphasis on institutional subordination and the complete effacement of women. The hierarchy may be explained as the visual imagining of a sequence of teaching. I can see no way to justify the effacement of women. For now, I will set Dionysius to one side, because what I wanted from him (or perhaps her—though that would make the irony in this corpus too complex even for me)—what I want from the Dionysian writings is the notion that theological negation is completed in care. I want to emphasize that principle and then to note its converse: pastoral care is incomplete without theological negation, not least when dealing with what we so glibly call morals.

Negative Moral Theology

I F NEGATIVE THEOLOGY is comprehensive soul care, how can it be confined by a subdivided theology just to topics in dogmatics or systematics? It cannot, but you will often find attempts to keep it there. The challenge of negative theology will be taken up, if it is not waved away, during discussions of theological method or human knowledge or divine simplicity. Negative theology is typically and I think deliberately not mentioned in typical prologues to Catholic moral theology or Evangelical Christian ethics.[3]

It is not hard to understand why most Christian ethicists want to keep negative theology at bay. First, negative theology appears to abolish ethics by a blunt rejection of "exceptionless norms" or, to speak in English, of universal regulations. Negative theology would produce anarchy, and nothing agitates these ethicists like the scent of anarchy. Again, it is hard to see how negative theology could contribute to what many take as the chief task of moral theology or Christian ethics; namely, framing those universal regulations and then applying them to particular cases. After all, ethicists are supposed to tell us what we can and can't do, aren't they? Finally, negative theology sounds terribly obscure, whereas Christian ethics must be clear—clear above all—otherwise, you won't know what you can and can't do.

There are replies to each of these worries, but let me reply to them together. If our speech about God is gripped tightly by the limits of human language, so too is our language about human beings as creatures who are in the image and likeness of God, who were created for a share in the inmost life of the Trinity. So long as pastoral care means to hasten the journey of human beings to their trinitarian home, the language of pastoral care must recognize itself as afflicted by our inability to describe that Trinity, to narrate its presence in human hearts, to capture the ways it draws human beings to itself. The language of practical theology falls fully under the event or operation of negative theology because human life cannot be narrated except in relation to the unnarratable life of God.

Near love, language ignites or evaporates. When the ablest Christian writers attempt to narrate their loving encounters with God, they do so by falling back on the incandescent languages of erotic passion. There are at least three obvious reasons for this. First, our encounters with God are intense, overwhelming experiences of love, and so we turn to the most compelling languages humans have devised for such experiences. Second, and as we have seen, piercing human love already undoes human language—already breaks the grip holding it closed. We fracture language for erotic love; when we need fractured language to talk about God, we pick up language already fractured. Third, more provocatively, it seems that the closest analogy in human experience to divine encounter really is erotic union. Ps-Dionysius goes out of his way to rescue the word *eros* for Christian use, precisely in comparison with *agape*.[4] I conclude from this and the other reasons that there can be no approach to a language for divine love except through the discourses of *eros*. I conclude that any adequate language for the love in Christian communities must be ultimately erotic.

You see how negative theology reforms the projects of moral theology or Christian ethics. Moral writing should be a form of exhortation always ready to drop its temporary descriptions and rules as soon as a believer begins to move through them toward God. The speech of Christian ethics may sometimes have to speak of laws, cases, clear conclusions, but it can do so only on the way to something it cannot formulate clearly as law—indeed, that it cannot formulate at all. A negative moral theology might rather begin not from laws and cases, but from persons in love—or rather from the pictures it paints of persons, from the identities it projects unto them. Persons carry the narrative of movement toward God. That movement is the whole concern of Christian moral theology. When there are fundamental slips in moral theology, they are likely to begin in the projection of personal identities.

The sort of slip I mean can be seen, for example, in theology's too eager use of reductive psychologies, especially in pastoral care. Of course such psychologies can be helpful in some ways, for given times. Of course they have brought consolation to suffering souls—not to say, uncertain pastors. Still, as necessarily limited and occasionally pernicious descriptions and explanations, reductive psychologies should be picked up by the theologian hesitantly, with a strong conviction of their incompleteness.[5] Christian ethics should retell such psychological models only when accompanied by the reminder that their negation would be a truer description of a psyche that is being treated intimately by the trinitarian God.

The grossest mistakes in the theological thinking of persons, and the most damaging, come from mistaking how loves enter into a person's life. Theology will misjudge not only which kinds of love are good, but also how particular loves define or determine the person feeling them. More specifically, great mistakes come from failing to see how *eros* is connected to moral identities. I can show this most helpfully from an extended example. The example is the projection of our most familiar identities for same-sex desire. I try to show how the process of negative theology might begin to correct church teaching about what we now call *homosexuality*.

A Negative Theology of Sexual Identities

ONE PLACE TO START with the effects of negative theology on same-sex identities would be by a simple denial: the negation of the label "homosexual" is truer in theologically important ways than its affirmation. Negating the identity "homosexual" does not mean applying instead its dialectical twin, the identity "heterosexual." "Heterosexual" is not the real or default position; it operates in tandem with "homosexual" at the same level of superficiality, in the same regime of clinical and political management. Negating the identity "homosexual" means something more like remembering what imposing that identity leaves out. Hear this carefully. Often when people say, "You're more than your homosexual identity," they seem to mean, "Please give up or hide your homosexual identity so that I can accept the rest."

I mean something different by negating the identity "homo-sexual." I mean denying its adequacy as a term for capturing the erotic passion of persons. This label for a sexual orien-tation—not to speak of the notion of sexual orientation it-self—is too crude, too silly, to capture what God has done underneath it.

I suggested a few paragraphs back that negative moral the-ology might be better off trying to understand the imposition of identities rather than the construction of principles and their application to cases. This is particularly important when it comes to sexual matters. The famously successful projection of sexual identities in Christian pastoral practice has produced a whole troupe of figures: the Sodomite, of course, but also the Lascivious Widow, the Witch, and the Self-Abuser, who was a figure of theological imagination be-fore he—less often, she—was an object of clinical attention. Against such sin identities, we could place sexual grace iden-tities, such as the Angelic Monk, the Virgin Martyr, the Chaste Wife, and the Priest with Pure Hands. Some of us may well laugh at such figures now, though it is important to remember that they are still performed daily right around us in Christian communities. Certainly, they are around my home in Atlanta, where the Sodomite is a recurring figure on "evangelical" radio. Christian moral theology has built re-markably durable identities around the prohibition of erotic lives.

In fact, I believe that such identities are performed in their variations where we least expect them. Beginning with the coining of the term *homosexual* about 130 years ago, most Eu-ropean and American gay identities still react against old churchly and civic persecution, against the terrors of Chris-tendom. Reaction determines not just some features of the identities, but more importantly what it means even to have a sex identity—that is, the very logic of the category. Contemporary gay identities become essences because their predecessors were persecuted as essences. The identities feel immutable because they were so often declared incorrigible.

Gay and lesbians may still need to debate from these identities in political spheres in order to secure or defend basic civic rights. The arguments that seem most convincing in American lobbying assume that nonheterosexual people are stamped out in identical shapes, just the way heterosexuals are presumed to be. (If heterosexuals weren't identically stamped out by machines well segregated from the queer-stamping machines, then heterosexuals might occasionally find their identities a little blurry, might find themselves from time to time ... No!) We who live through being gay or lesbian may even need to inhabit fixed identities for a while in church debates before we can set to work dismantling them. But then, before too many more repetitions, we need to apply negative theology to the roles we inhabit in order to be heard.

Negative theology is risky for the afflicted. It can easily become yet another means of rendering them voiceless. At the same time, it is an unequaled tool for cutting away churchly ideologies on their own terms. To say this risk in another way: negative theology can appear to discount the desire for recognition by those on the margins. "Your self and its material concerns are petty. You need to transcend them into more spiritual concerns (while leaving my privileges intact)." At the same time, negation can free those who have been assigned stigmatizing identities. So, if we must be careful about when or before whom we apply negative theology on our own stigmata, we must still apply it. Our most thoughtful speeches cannot end with fixed identities, with mechanical reactions to the old persecutions. We have to take these reactions apart in hopes of seeing what we might possibly do on our own, not in reaction. I come to those possibilities in a moment. I want now to emphasize consequences of negating the category "homosexual."

My comments on the history and logic of this identity can sound like a version of what gets dismissed as "social construction." They are. Some versions of social construction are trustworthy guides to a negative moral theology of same-sex identities. The "constructionist" account takes up one argument from Foucault's *History of Sexuality* 1. For Foucault, the appearance in the nineteenth century of a series of new names for sexual "perversions" marked the elaboration of a new set of categories, of identities, for classifying human sexual life.[6] The center of these new categories was the very notion of perversion itself, which was incessantly subdivided into greater and lesser types. One of the greater types was the "homosexual," who was followed only tardily by the "heterosexual," itself originally a perversion—that is, an excessive erotic fixation on members of the opposite sex.[7]

To say that these categories were invented in the nineteenth century is not to say that there were no same-sex dispositions, desires, or acts before that nineteenth century. Nor does it imply that we couldn't impose nineteenth-century categories of perversion retrospectively. Of course we could—we impose identities retrospectively all the time and all over time. The constructionist caution is rather that the people who had those dispositions or desires, who committed those acts, didn't describe themselves using the category "homosexual"—which hadn't yet been invented. Nor were they so described by other people who were denouncing, capturing, imprisoning, and executing them. Our categories for describing human erotic lives—or rather the categories prescribed by our authorities—are not themselves natural or timeless. Contemporary labels have specific genealogies and are imbedded in all too aggressive programs of social control.

What lies underneath the labels from the nineteenth century now used in Christian theology? There is no natural, timeless, universal language in which to reply to such a question. We couldn't say what lies underneath our labels even if we had a precise genetic explanation of the physical bases of different same-sex desires or impulses, because those desires or impulses will be experienced, articulated, practiced, interpreted, and judged within some particular historical genealogy of culture or religion. The enormous range of erotic behavior between women or between men—genital and nongenital, repeated or singular, named or anonymous, acknowledged or repressed, in varying numbers, postures, costumes, places, and times—this *eros* appears in daily life already constructed into identities by languages, moral codes, races, classes, cultures, and religions, each of them changing over time. This is what social construction suggests, and its suggestion helps us to perform negative theology on same-sex identities that now so preoccupy Christian moralists.

As we perform the negation, we are led toward another— the negation of theology's own uncritical history. So far as Christian moral theology and pastoral practice have failed to negate their own identity categories, they have gotten same-sex desire wrong. They got it wrong as a category and as an object of pastoral concern. Who will seriously maintain that Christian pastoral practice toward "sodomites" of 500 years ago or toward "homosexuals" 100 or 50 years ago had an adequate account of life with same-sex desire?

The pastoral care of persons with same-sex desires has a history. The history includes horrors, from which we should not turn away. My point is that the horrors were authorized by dangerous conceptual mistakes—mistakes about sins, of course, but more deeply mistakes about erotic identities. We ought by now to be able to say that the identities projected by pastoral theology around same-sex desires were dangerously wrong. We don't say this because we now have superior knowledge. We say it because we have superior ignorance, ignorance that knows itself to be ignorance. Indeed, negative theology would suggest that the fundamental rule of pastoral care with regard to same-sex desire would be the inadequacy of any theological projection of an identity that has been done up till now—or that is likely to be done in the near future.

From this negation of projected identities, we might be able to take one or two more steps into this example of negative moral theology. One step would be to recognize that the inadequacy of the pastoral identities projected around sex does not imply that Christianity has only a weak power to project those identities. On the contrary, Christianity's power to project one identity after another, to invent a new one just as the old breaks apart, to swap scripts with various secular powers, suggests that the Christian pastorate retains a striking power over these identities. Christian churches have been able to project sin identities not only because of their political power in certain regions, but because of essential features of their doctrine and worship. Christian churches ought still to retain some of that power over identities—despite their diminished political standing in industrialized nations and their more and more noticeable vulnerability in the face of mass cultures.

My pious hope is that this power might be used to counterbalance the sex identities projected by increasingly powerful systems for managing sex, systems of the modern state and of the mass media. Indeed, I also hope—here you see how sweetly pious I remain—that Christian practical theology might open the way for new ways of being erotic. It might be able to speak of something outside of the kinds of identity we have known—not another identity, but a kind of erotic desire beyond punitive or "liberatory" identities altogether.

We reach the second step, the last I want to make in illustrating the application of negative theology to pastoral care. Beyond all the particular mistakes of moral theology in regard to sexual identities, I find a recurring mistake in Christianity about the power of the erotic. To call it a mistake misleads. It is more the pretense of a false certainty—the anxious declaration of a solution to a disturbing ambivalence. The ambivalence can be seen in classical mystical doctrine. On the one hand, sexual desire is something to be mastered at the lowest level of spiritual progress. Sexual desire is brought under control, as regards both actions and willed thoughts, early on in "purgation." On the other hand, the only language useful for describing the highest levels of spiritual life in this life, the near approach of God, is highly eroticized language. Whether it is an allegorical reading of the Song of Songs or metaphors of fiery piercing and tender embrace, Christian speech cannot do without erotic words, including words that bend gender expectations in the oddest ways. These words are not metaphors. They constitute the best language we have, maybe the only language we have, for talking about union with God.

The erotic helps us to conceive the original and persisting force of our ascent to the divine. It is in us what responds to grace. It is our deepest experience of grace—of the grace that kindles and directs desire.[8] So, while the process of negative theology on the pastoral care of the erotic undoes our never adequate projection of sexual identities, it opens space for more serious talk about the erotic. Not that we could ever describe it, define it, capture it, reduce it to principles under which to decide cases. Of course not. Perhaps we might yet learn to talk about it otherwise than by anxiously dismissing it—and then returning to it rapturously behind closed doors

The quarrel in the churches over sex is not mainly an issue of justice, though it is certainly that. It is not just an imperative to correct dangerous pastoral mistakes, though it is that, too. The reason why we must quarrel over pastoral care for erotic life until the end—beyond the end—is that the erotic touches the core of our desire for God, which is the heart of our Christian life. If the churches changed all their antihomoerotic policies overnight—now that would be a miracle!—we would still need to think about why the churches had got the policies wrong for so many centuries. Because we would still need the queer violation of Christian pastoral categories as a reminder of how easy it is to make pastoral mistakes about the erotic—and how urgent it is to reverse them. I am even willing to carry the stigma of being this hypereroticized being who is your author, this sex-obsessed dissident who causes scandal to the faithful, for the sake of reminding how important it is to tell truth about our erotic attraction to God.

The Form of a Negative Theology of the Erotic

YOU MAY BY NOW be saying to yourself, Wasn't this supposed to be a chapter about telling God? It has been. I have argued that erotic language is indispensable in describing what pulls us toward God, what directs us to our created end. Still, I want to address this question more generally in this final, short segment of the chapter—and the segment is short indeed. In it, I name at last this chapter's form.

The argument of negative theology is that we fail radically

in naming God or capturing God's operation in human speech. The proposal of negative theology is to apply a process of negation, to stage an event of denial at every point in Christian theology, in order to hasten the union of believers with God. I have tried to illustrate the argument from theological treatments of the erotic, as I have applied the process of negation to one of the Christian erotic identities, namely, same-sex identities. But how is this naming God?

An immediate answer would be that we name God from what God reveals to us and does in us. Puzzles in scriptural language were the starting point of negative theology for Ps-Dionysius, and narratives of divine action in human history or community were its way forward. So, talking about God's action on our erotic passion is talking about God—as it is pursuing a program of negative theology. But by now it must be clear that this immediate answer is misleading when it assumes that we can readily identify what God does in our erotic passions as distinct from what our erotic passions themselves do. I am not saying there is no grace. I am suggesting that we may not recognize grace in *eros* because we have been taught to see it as merely erotic. "That can't be grace, because that is my desire."

There is a second and more interesting answer to the question, How is this chapter about naming God? The process of negative theology strips away the pretensions of our proudest language about God. It does this in part by rehabilitating our humblest language about God. Our humblest language about God is the language that doesn't even insist upon claims to God's action. It may be that the most cunning negative theology would give up the appearance of theology altogether.[9] In disputing about the adequacy of the prevailing sexual identities; in resisting the pressures of managed sexuality in government, the churches, or "health care";

in striving to fracture sexual distinctions through protest or parody, we may be preparing our language for its most intimate encounter with God—without ever using the proud title "theology."

Finally, the most interesting answer to the question, How has all of this been about naming God? Speech about God is best done as speech to God, who is present through scriptural texts and the actions of grace, who entices and supports at every point the motion through language to God's own life. So, the privileged form of Christian speech, including the speech of practical theology, is prayer.

You may understand this as prayer of petition. Certainly, practical theology ought to write down its petitions for fuller understanding—which will be less positive understanding. It ought to pray for not stopping short, for not seeking completion in words. It might even be willing to pray for truth telling as confession of what it understands to have happened even as it feels fully that it does not understand. At moments of strongest disagreement, Christian writers might even be willing to pray in public for patience and peace—patience and peace without the hope of any final resolution in words.

You may better understand the prayer of moral or practical theology—of any theology—as the prayer of contemplation. The shapes for writing negative theology encourage or stage a rush into the encounter with God. That flight desires God, depends on God, supposes God for its first desire. So, the forms for writing theology enact a prayer. A prayer that does not keep official secrets or silence uncomfortable voices; a prayer that is neither glib piety nor societal nostalgia; a prayer that has no familiar certainties, that does not ratify church power or collaborate with state control; still a prayer, a prayer that reaches with hottest desire through soberest mind to embrace.

You may best understand the prayer of moral or practical theology—of any theology—as the prayer of someone who is never captured by a prescribed identity. Prayer may become—it ought to be—one speech in which we do not have to perform the scripts according to our sexual orientations, our gender or sex, our centrality or marginality. Consider this possibility as the future contribution of negative theology to liturgy, among many other things.

This chapter is an exhortation to prayer. It is like the call, "Let us pray." An exhortation to prayer doesn't end with the end of the call. We continue to be exhorted. We will be exhorted even more—and shown how and to whom to pray —when the unspeakable God of our desires takes flesh and talks.

TELLING G⊕D'S BODY
THE FLESH OF INCARNATION

T HE AUTHOR we have labeled "Pseudo-Dionysius" sketches the mystical "ascent" and then turns "downward" into language about the churches. In the same way, I turn from reflections on negative theology in relation to God to the more demanding case, which is talk about Jesus. I want to gather together questions and possibilities from the previous chapters for thinking about Jesus' body. His body is the beginning of Christian truth telling and also the point at which the fragmentation of our languages finds hope, not of unification, but of enlivening.

For many contemporary speakers, telling the truth about Jesus means finding the "real" or "historical" Jesus underneath the stories and theologies constructed around him. The truth about Jesus, they affirm, is the truth about what he really said and did as opposed to what various Christian communities made of him. So, telling the truth about Jesus' body would mean reminding listeners that he was a Jewish peasant who did manual labor rather than an Anglo-Saxon movie star surrounded by a constant halo tweaked by a diffusion filter. The best way to represent the historical truth about Jesus' body would be to reconstruct a composite or typical portrait of a Nazarene who was born around the beginning of the common era. Just that kind of portrait was constructed for a recent television series, and the composite image circulated widely in the press.[1]

Much can be said for and against that kind of truth about Jesus. On the one hand, it challenges easy suppositions about how we got from Jesus to the churches. Jesus was not a blond screen idol, and he did not go about preaching treatises on the union of divine and human natures in himself. On the other hand, the present search for the historical Jesus supposes both that the experience of an incarnate God must be like any other experience and that texts recording that experience must be like any other texts. It also supposes, at least in some of its versions, that no god could become human in the way theological traditions have supposed. These are curious suppositions and commitments, but my concern at the moment is not to engage them. I want to ask another sort of question—a question based on a hypothesis. The hypothesis is this: whoever Jesus was "in reality," the most important fact about him is that he was a good and perhaps the best way for God to become human. The question follows: if Jesus' body was God's body, how do we begin to tell truths about it?

A devotee of the current pursuit of the historical Jesus might object immediately that my question simply repeats the deviation of the Christian tradition. By hypothesizing that Jesus of Nazareth was God incarnate, I am superimposing the "high Christology" of the Gospel of John onto the much different facts about Jesus that we can discover in hypothesized proto-Gospels or reconstructed oral traditions. My reply is to repeat more fully what I said earlier: the aim of this chapter is not to pit assumption against assumption or method against method. The chapter asks a question on the basis of a hypothesis. If you want, you can think of it as a thought experiment. At the very least, the thought experiment will clarify difficulties of speech in contemporary churches—because in fact the churches find it awkward to talk fully about the implications of the high Christology, that is, of the affirmation of incarnation. Truth telling is not the same as reconstructing facts according to the reigning "common sense." Certainly, telling the truth about Jesus requires at least talking about the disconcerting consequences of the traditional affirmations that God took flesh.[2]

The most familiar Christian creeds or confessions, for all of their polemical contingency and philosophical complication, profess the religion of an incarnate God. Their words are repeated in so many Christian liturgies that it seems silly to refer to them. Hear in your memory's ear at least some phrases from an English "Nicene Creed": "Who for us men, and for our salvation, came down from heaven; and was incarnate by the Holy Ghost of the Virgin Mary, and was made man." Or, in a less aggressively masculinist translation: "Who for us human beings, and for our salvation, descended from heaven, and was put into flesh by the holy spirit from the virgin, Mary, and became human." "Incarnate," "put into flesh." Some Christians kneel or bow their heads at the words. Most know them by rote. Christianity as the religion of God in human flesh—it is almost too trite to say and yet still too disconcerting to think.[3]

Roman Catholicism in particular prides itself on being a strongly incarnational practice of Christianity. The sacramental theater of Catholic liturgy culminates when God becomes flesh in bread and wine. We Catholics profess to believe that it is the actual body of Jesus, back among us. Indeed, we preserve unconsumed pieces in tabernacles. Images of the Catholic Jesus are its lesser manifestations. The image body hovers over our churches in graphic crucifixes, in prints of the Sacred Heart, in scourged statues of the Man of Sorrows. Then the body of Jesus raised from the dead: "Do not touch me," he says to Mary Magdalene, "for I have not yet ascended to the Father" (John 20:17). That single sentence has inspired or provoked dozens of master paintings. The body of Jesus is mirrored in the bodies of his saints, whose relics are venerated and whose martyrdoms or miracles take contours in church art. The events around Jesus' body are also reperformed more straightforwardly. When I was a boy in central Mexico, a young man was chosen to take on the role of Christ during Holy Week. His body became the image of Christ's body. It rode into the dusty recreation of Jerusalem, there to celebrate the meal, to be arrested and scourged, to be tried and condemned. On the afternoon of Good Friday, the young man's body was tied up on a cross.

Alongside these rites and artifacts, Roman Catholics have also cultivated certain ways of meditating on the incarnate God. The meditations picture the body of Jesus at many moments and under different aspects. We have from famous theologians sustained reflections on Jesus as an infant or at the age of twelve, Jesus in desert retreat or preaching on the mount. Ignatius of Loyola asks us to imagine Jesus as a noble commander so that we will respond by joining up.[4] Most famously, theologians and spiritual masters write of Jesus in the days of his Passion: the body of Jesus going down to death. The "Stations of the Cross" is only one of hundreds of texts about Jesus' body that aims to produce compunction through compassion.

Doctrines, liturgies, icons, and meditations about Christ's body teach many things about it, but hardly everything. There are ambiguities and absences. Indeed, the absences are marked by ambiguities. Consider the ambiguities around the "simple fact" that Jesus' body was male. God incarnate as a human being has to fall somewhere within the range of human sex differentiation, and that range is often reduced by our societies to a dichotomy: male *or* female. So, we know about Jesus' body that it must have had some sex, and we accept it as historical fact that the sex was (unambiguously!) male. We also know that it has been very important for most Christian churches that his body was male. Jesus' maleness has been used to justify a number of theological conclusions, as it is still used by some churches to exclude women from ministry. For these churches, it is not trivial that Jesus was marked as male from his birth.

Christian traditions consider it important that Jesus was a male, both because he needed some sex/gender and because he had the sex/gender that claims particular privileges and powers. Christian traditions haven't often considered it important to reflect on what made Jesus male—that is, on the fact that the incarnate God had genitals of a certain configuration. Indeed, and as you may have felt in reading that last sentence, the genitals of Jesus are typically and normatively excluded from speech. To talk about them is indecent or provocative or blasphemous. To meditate on them would be obscene. We are urged to meditate on Jesus' acts and sufferings. We are asked to gaze on imaginary portraits of him and picture for ourselves his height and weight, the color of his skin or the length of his hair. But if our meditation should drift downward toward his pelvis, we are immediately rebuked and then condemned as perverted or pornographic.

Reflect on the vehemence of those rebukes and condemnations. Reflect on it and then push back against it. Our meditations on Jesus are incomplete without his sex. Telling the truth about him, we ought to try to tell it whole. But there is more: a vehement refusal to think Jesus' sex while insisting on his masculinity suggests that we have yet to tell an anxious truth *about ourselves* in relation to Jesus' body. We are not able even to speak about some parts of it. Why is that?

There follows a meditation on the body of the incarnate God. It meditates on the part of that body that is both necessary and unspeakable, that is fetishized and hidden. So, it becomes a meditation on our needs in relation to that body. The aim of the meditation is to make us more capable of telling a truth that we cannot. We need the truth, and we are afraid of it.

Meditations on Christ take many forms, but they often permit themselves graphic and impassioned speech. I have given myself that permission here. Please do not confuse it with the presumption of propositional language that imagines itself capturing God.

Jesus' Corpses

MUCH CHRISTIAN theology claims to be about a divine incarnation. It is also, and perhaps more emphatically, a speech for managing that incarnation by controlling its awkward implications. Some particularly awkward consequences can only be managed by passing over members of the body of God in prudish silence. Looked at in this way, the history of Christian theology can be seen as a long flight from the full consequences of its central profession. The big business of theology has been to construct alternate bodies for Jesus the Christ—tidier bodies, bodies better conformed to institutional needs. I think of these artificial bodies as Jesus' corpses, and I consider large parts of official Christology their mortuary.

Take as an emblem for the management of this awkward incarnation a typical Catholic crucifix. On it, a man wearing a loincloth is nailed. The representation is "realistic": the muscles on the body are sharply defined, nails poke through the strained skin, and the head lolls to one side in agony or exhaustion. If the crucifix before us is an older one from southern European or Latin American churches, the "realism" will be greater still. Vividly red blood runs over creamy skin—runs down from a minutely crafted crown of thorns, from nail punctures, from a bruised and swollen cut just below the ridge of ribs. The face itself is in full agony, with beseeching eyes and a moaning or screaming mouth. The depiction is strikingly and perhaps appallingly realistic. Or is it? On one antique Mexican crucifix that hung in my mother's home, a corpus of this kind bore only a flimsy bit of parchment as its loincloth. When the paper fell away after one too many moves, it was revealed that there was nothing underneath. The corpus on the crucifix was shockingly detailed, except in the lower abdomen, which was as smooth and abstract as an old-fashioned manikin.

Imagine for a moment a more completely incarnate practice of carving crucifixes. The carver would take special care to carve equally realistic genitals on each corpus, whether or not a miniature loincloth would soon hide the work. The genitals would be considered—as they were in some periods of Christian painting—a powerful sign of the fullness of incarnation.[5] The penis would be circumcised in conformity with scriptural evidence and as a sign of Jesus' obedience to Jewish law. But it would be neither exaggerated nor minimized, fetishized neither as a commodity to be chased nor as a disgrace to be repudiated. We might even imagine a tradition of special prayers or meditations for attending to this extraordinary consequence of an eternal God's love for us perishable creatures, who must reproduce to survive as bodies. The genitals would be carved reverently as a profound teaching inscribed on the surface of the body of God-with-us.

To my knowledge, we Catholics have not had such a tradition for carving crucifixes. On the contrary, we have expected, when we have not required, that genitals be left off a crucifix's corpus, no matter how "realistic." We have also traditionally insisted that Jesus not be shown naked in paintings of the crucifixion. At various times, nakedness on the cross has been explicitly refused even though it was conceded to be more historically accurate.[6] Jesus most probably was naked on the cross, but we cannot show him that way. You can catch here not only a curious disregard for history, but a refusal to accept divine providence. God did not prevent what Catholic art wants to prohibit. God let Jesus hang naked on the cross; our crucifixes cannot. Indeed, and with few exceptions, Catholic art has refused to allow any hint of a penis underneath Jesus' loincloth. The loincloth must cover a vacuum.[7]

Nothing underneath the loincloth—take that as an emblem for our thought about Jesus' body. The loincloth is not so much a rag as a magic cloth that makes things disappear. Why do we need the magic? That is a complicated question, to which I give several answers. The first of them begins this way: ask yourself what you have been feeling while reading through the last half dozen paragraphs. Is it recognition and insight? Calm and reasoned rejection? Or have you perhaps been feeling some distaste, embarrassment, disgust, repulsion? Have you been feeling that His genitals shouldn't be talked about—much less imagined as seen? If so, you may understand that we need that loincloth to keep ourselves from being ashamed. The cloth covers part of Jesus, which means that it helps us not to look at ourselves. His loincloth is made to cover our eyes.

Here is the beginning of a second answer: imagine, again, the tradition for carving detailed genitals onto each and every crucifix. Who is doing the carving? If it is a woman, she might be presumed (in a male-centered theology at least) to be sexually aroused by such detailed attention to images of a penis—unless, of course, she is presumed not to know anything about them. If the carver is a man, he is supposed to be entirely disinterested in the genitals—except that the soul of every believer is Christ's spouse, is as a bride to Jesus considered as spiritual bridegroom. It might even be in some rare cases, in the overheated workshop of an undisciplined monastery, that a pious male carver would begin to find the carving of those members oddly—no, we cannot begin to think that. It is not enough to cover them up. We have to prevent their being carved in the first place. Think of the scandal to (and from) the carvers.

On many traditional readings, sexual shame began in Eden after the fall into sin. "Then the eyes of both were naked: and they sewed fig leaves together and made loincloths for themselves" (Genesis 3:7). Adam and Eve made loincloths because they had sinned. Why do we make loincloths for our images of Jesus, in statues or in paintings? Because *we* sin. We have to cover him up because of what we have become in our fearful denials. Certainly it's not God who is ashamed of human genitals—or God who pulls back from the shame meant to be inflicted on Jesus by crucifying him naked. We are the ones ashamed both of human bodies as created and of what we do to human bodies when we want to humiliate them. We are afraid of how we might respond to a naked savior. We are afraid of what we do to each other when we use nakedness as an insult.[8]

For the most traditional theology, it would be a sign of full redemption to represent Jesus naked on the cross.[9] His nakedness would be a sign of a redeemed—that is, a humanly mature—community of believers. But we are afraid to look at the body of God as it was. So, our typical "Jesus"—as corpus, statue, painting—only adds to the series of Jesus' corpses. The corpses are mutilated. We cannot let Jesus' body be whole, either in death or in life.

Jesus' Sex and Jesus' Gender

CHRISTIAN TRADITIONS have wanted to hide on Jesus' body the organs of male sex at the same time that they have wanted to insist upon his male gender. A full consideration of this division might look to the difference between male organ and male power, between what theorists distinguish as the penis and the phallus. The penis is an organ while the phallus is a totem. I propose for the moment only the beginning of a simpler analysis. Consider how the distinction between sex and gender in Jesus allows his masculinity to be pliable for official purposes.

Two cautions before beginning this consideration. First, the distinction between sex and gender can only be provisional. The distinction has been used to separate (physically determined) sex from (culturally constructed) gender. *Sex* means roughly the kind of body you are born with. *Gender* is the way you were taught to handle that sexed body within a certain social regime. Between *sex* and *gender* there appears *sexuality*, which sometimes seems physiologically based and cross-cultural, at other times culturally specific and always under construction. But the trichotomy, the triplet of terms, cannot be stable. It is never clear, for example, what should be included in *gender*. Analyzed carefully, *sex* is no less troublesome, since external genital anatomy is only one biological marker of sex and since societies disagree when interpreting the marker. So, in distinguishing Jesus' (hidden) sex from Jesus' (institutionalized) gender, we can only expect a rough-and-ready distinction between what cannot be cleanly separated.

The second caution: in talking about Jesus' gender, it is safest not to get entangled in questions about his "sexual orientation." It is very useful to undo the heterosexist presumption that Jesus was of course heterosexual—that he would obviously have been married to a woman if he had entered into an erotic relation at all. As incarnate God, Jesus violated any number of social expectations. Perhaps he would have violated this one, too. Of course, the deceptions in applying terms for sexual orientation across history are numerous even when there is an abundance of evidence. There is little or no evidence about Jesus' sexual desires in the canonical Gospels.[10] So, while it is helpful to rethink the Gospel narratives without the assumption that Jesus was "heterosexual," it is very wise not to attempt to prove that he was "homosexual." In any case, the point here is not to inaugurate a quest for the historical Jesus' sexuality. The point is to notice the consequences of how Christian traditions have distinguished Jesus' sex from Jesus' gender.

Recall again the contrast between silence on sex and stridency on gender. When canonical theologians have considered Jesus' sex, they have refused to allow it what might be considered ordinary sexual operations. Reasoning from hypotheses about genitals in Eden before the fall, and from rules about the right use of sex, they have suggested, for example, that Jesus never had an erection. Erections in Eden would have been voluntary: Adam would have chosen to have one only for purposes of procreation with Eve. Since Jesus never willed to copulate with anyone, he would not have willed an erection.[11] Again, the disorder of human sexual desire is considered both a cause and an effect of original sin. When I feel the rush of desire for another man, I am only showing that I am objectively disordered in consequence of the sin that long ago disrupted human life. When a heterosexual woman feels lust for a man whom she never intends to marry and without any notion of procreative possibilities, she too is showing disorder. Jesus was not disordered by sin. So,

Jesus didn't suffer such desires. In sum, for many traditional Christian theologies, Jesus had genitals (which need to be hidden), but he did not have anything like what we think of as ordinary sexual reactions. He was like us in all things but sin—and the traditions stigmatize most of our experienced sexuality as sin.

So far, the enforced silence on Jesus' sex. The strident affirmations of Jesus' gender are much more familiar to us. We Catholics hear, for example, that women can't be ordained to priesthood because they cannot represent or symbolize Jesus. We are told, again, that church leadership is more appropriate to men than to women: not only was Jesus himself a man, but he chose only men as his disciples. So, Jesus' masculine gender has enormous significance for church life. Indeed, recent Vatican arguments against the ordination of women suppose that the maleness of priesthood is a divine given that cannot be changed by the church even if it wanted to.[12]

Of course, Jesus' masculinity is somewhat curious. First, most Christian churches have conceived it as a strictly celibate masculinity, since they take it as obvious that Jesus never engaged in sexual activity. Second, though perhaps less obviously, Jesus' masculinity is a sort of eunuch masculinity. If we are to believe that he never "had sex," we are also not to think about his having male organs for sex. Finally, the masculinity of male Christian leaders has often itself strained social expectations of masculinity. In the Catholic Church, the normatively celibate priesthood has not infrequently been treated as a sort of third sex or intersex. It has been assigned gender roles that mix or confuse ordinary gender expectations. There are, I suspect, similar shifts of gender expectations even in the normatively married Protestant clergy. So, while Jesus' masculinity is held up as the standard for the masculinity of Christian ministry, it is also complicated in ways that make it seem problematically masculine.

If believing Christians hesitate to accuse Jesus of being effeminate, they have not hesitated to level the accusation against particular representations of him. Bruce Barton, once popular as author of *The Man Nobody Knows* (to be read with emphasis on "man"), was pushed to portray Jesus as an athletic business leader because he was so put off by representations of Jesus as a wimp.[13] If the prevailing images of Jesus were not to be abandoned altogether, they had to be monitored quite closely. Consider Warner Sallman's best-selling portraits of Christ.[14] Sallman himself undertook them precisely in order in present the figure of a masculine Christ, a "real" man's Christ. Alas, Sallman himself was accused of presenting a soft, strange, effeminate Christ, with glistening locks and flimsy robes. So, the pictures of Jesus have to be toughened up, butched up. Jesus' portraits have to keep proving their masculinity.

What threatens the masculinity of Jesus' representations? I've mentioned earlier some reasons why Jesus' official masculinity is problematic from the start, but I should add here another reason we can notice particularly in portraits. Religious images are objects of devotion. Jesus' masculinity must be troubled because both men and women have passionate and psychologically intimate relations to him. His portraits are meant to attract and direct devotion. They are portraits of someone loved ardently by members of both sexes.

Jesus is our Lord, but also our friend. We go to him with our cares and our concerns. We suppose that he knows all of our shameful secrets, including our hidden sexual desires and acts. He even sees us performing them. So, Jesus knows things about my body and what I do with it that an erotic partner of many years may not know, that the sum of my lovers may not have seen. Jesus knows me inside out. He loves me and I love him. He wants to help me in my daily struggle to live rightly, including with regard to sexual desires and acts. How does his gaze on my body affect my gaze on his? How does the intimacy of our relationship trouble my relation to him as someone who has a sexed body? Must I hide his sex in part because I can't figure out how to think of his sex in relation to our intimacy, my devotion? For heterosexual men, Jesus must be a buddy and cannot be only a buddy (since Jesus sees private things a buddy isn't supposed to see). For nonheterosexual men, Jesus can all too easily be more than a buddy—with the dangers that implies. What is it for a "straight" woman to have a superbly attractive man solicit her deepest love even as he knows her intimate history? And if lesbians might seem to escape the paradoxes of reacting with desire to Jesus' physical body, they might seem to be especially subjected to his (male) gaze. Every human body is watched by Jesus everywhere it goes, in everything it does. Is it any wonder that we are so worried about how Jesus appears—and must not appear?[15]

Other reactions to portraits of Jesus are not only possible, but certainly more frequent in conscious experience. I may look at a crucifix and think that it is bad art, a bit of factory kitsch. Or I may look at it and recall how different Jesus may have looked "in fact." Or, again, the sight of a crucifix may lead me to meditate on the many ways in which Jesus appears to me—in the consecrated bread and wine, in the faces of the needy, in the luminous transfigurations of human love. Jesus' physical body may be noted more as absent or as multiplied than as singular and specific. Still, if I am led by a piece of religious art to place myself at the foot of the cross, to walk with Jesus on the road to Emmaus, to follow his commands in a fishing boat on Galilee, I must also meditate on my reaction to his body, which must be sexed as human bodies are.

Why need that confrontation be erotic, someone might ask? Isn't any effort to eroticize Jesus' body a sign more of cultural decadence than of serious thinking about faith? After all, isn't it a hypersexualized culture that forces us to consider every body in terms of its sex and to worry that every relation is repressed sexuality? There is a real point to these questions, and I will come back to it in a moment. I would only note now that anxieties over Jesus' sex or gender predate contemporary America. They predate the preoccupations of "muscular Christianity" and the YMCA. We have noticed already old quandaries about the representation of Jesus crucified. We could also have noted that Christians have always been attracted by an ideal of life beyond sex and have considered such a life an imitation of their Lord's life. Jesus' sex has always been unsettling, both cause and effect of how unsettling any sex has been for Christianity. We deduce our sexual morality from Jesus' rejected sex; Jesus must have rejected sex because of our sexual morality. So, we need not be afraid to stand by the insight that troubles about the sexed body of the Messiah are deeply inscribed in Christian living. They are not merely cultural byproducts of the last decades—or centuries. We should not be afraid to continue with our meditations.

Truth about the Body of God

WHAT IS IT to tell the truth about a human body? Is it the truth of a medical chart or an autopsy report? The body is described with its age and weight, medical conditions, signs of traumatic injury, or inward decay. The body is reported science. Or is the truth of a body more like a fashion spread in a glossy magazine? The body has been bathed and prepared with nameable products for its skin and hair, new perfumes and makeup colors. It has been regimented or surgically altered to the prevailing type. It will be further tailored with the photo software. The body is a billboard.

For Christians, the truth about Jesus' body would be neither of these—and not just because there was neither plastic surgery nor modern autopsy. The believer's truth about Jesus is always a truth told in love. How do you tell loving truths about a body? We sometimes pretend as if the most loving truth is a truth that lies about bodies by making them more attractive than they are—or than any body could be. Parents dote over their infant children, as those freshly in love gush about the unique and complete beauty of their new amours. We discount descriptions given by new parents and new lovers. To us, the infant looks pretty much like any other, and the new girlfriend or boyfriend has a funny nose and unconvincing hair. Love lies about bodies, we conclude. Or should we rather say: love discovers another way to talk about truths in bodies?

Some older Christian writers held, from reading Isaiah 53:2–3, that Jesus was in fact ugly.[16] Most Christian writers on the Passion have stressed that Jesus was made ugly on the cross. Some representations of the crucifixion seem to vie in representing his deformity—the twisting of the emaciated limbs, the gouges and tears in the flayed skin, or the inhuman agony of the jaundiced and bloodshot eyes. Often this sort of meditation has been linked to claims that Jesus' suffering was absolutely unique in its intensity, that he has suffered the woes of all humanity combined, and so on. I find it more helpful to think of Jesus on the cross as right in the middle of human suffering. Not everyone is executed in public for political or religious crimes, but then crucifixion is an easy way to go in comparison with many other forms of political and religious torture. So, I conclude not that Jesus' body on the cross was the most deformed body of suffering, but that it looked worse than some and better than others. Whatever suffering his body showed when it was taken down, other bodies have shown far worse.

What makes the ugliness of Jesus' crucified body important is not that it was the greatest physical ugliness, but that we are asked to see through it to the unspeakable beauty of God. The crucifixion inverts our ordinary bodily aesthetic by claiming that the radiant source of all beauty was disclosed to us in a scourged, crucified, dead body. Bonaventure says it succinctly: if you want to understand the presence of goodness in this world of bodies, there is no other way than by walking the streets of Jerusalem on the way to Golgotha.[17] Julian of Norwich describes it more graphically—too graphically for some readers. The head of Jesus, bleeding from its crown of thorns, is held over her while she suffers her own passion, and she looks up at it as most beautiful.[18]

Beautiful because desired, because loved? Both and neither. Paradoxical assertions about Jesus' beauty on the cross invite us to learn that bodies can be beautiful in ways we hadn't expected—or were perhaps afraid to think. A body can be beautiful even after rites of humiliation or pain not because those rites produce beauty, but because its beauty escapes those rites. How much more, then, might a loved body remain somehow beautiful no matter what. The height of sentimentality? Or an insight into the beauty that lies in human bodies being what they are? If the notion of the beauty of Jesus even when crucified is too much at present, or too suspiciously morbid, might we at least learn from it that a desired body can be complete, and so endowed with capacities for the erotic, even when it appears as ugly?

A tenacious student regularly objected to me in a class on Christianity and sexuality that *eros* couldn't fit with *agape* because *eros* was particular in two senses: it was directed at a specific object and it was choosy in its attractions.[19] I replied—I reply—that this is a polemical notion of *eros*. We are used to having our erotic tastes put into tiny packages for a number of opposed and collusive reasons: to keep them confined, to keep them out of sight, to make them amenable to marketing. How are you going to sell beauty as a commodity unless you can make *eros* a form of commodity fetishism? But couldn't we take *eros* out of those packages to think about how it might not be confined to particular notions of beauty or particular acts and objects? And shouldn't we do so if we regard Jesus' body as a teaching about embodiment in every one of its moments? He shows us a body in which desire is not only for the predictably beautiful and in which *eros* can outlast even well-calibrated humiliations.

In each moment, Jesus' body is a complete human body. Meditate on how to represent that. We need as an emblem for Jesus' body neither the unsexed corpus of a crucifix nor its necessary opposite—a body with gigantic genitals. We don't want to replace the mutilated corpse on the crucifix with a Christian version of one of the ancient satyr statues, in which the body is dwarfed by an engorged phallus. Indeed, our representations of Jesus' body should show us most vividly how a body can be erotic without being only or obsessively erotic. We should learn from it how a body has sex without being just sex. We learn this, not coincidentally, from a divine body that is unafraid to be naked even when it is supposedly humiliated. Here, Jesus trumps Nietzsche's Dionysus. Jesus is so divinely erotic that he need not be ashamed of either his "beauty" or his "ugliness." He is thus the god to teach us why our sexual shame really was a product of sin.

We should learn from the unashamed Jesus that our erotic reactions to him, whether we call him beautiful or ugly, are far from being a cause of shame. They are indispensable in our love of God. I am not thinking here again of the familiar and yet mysterious dependence of "mystical" language on the erotic.[20] Nor am I thinking of recent attempts to rediscover the sexuality latent in our theology of God.[21] No doubt our encounters with the divine must actualize our deepest capacities for joy and for intimacy, along with the highly charged sexual languages we have made to describe them. No doubt, too, our scriptures record how many ways our deepest psychological formations have projected themselves onto representations of God. We have in the incarnation not only a concession to our bodily life, but a vindication of it.

After all, and on the most traditional teaching, our bodies are not something we Christians expect to abandon with a relieved or desperate "Good riddance!" We get our bodies back again and stay with them for eternity. We get them back as the best human bodies there are, which means, as bodies with genitals. Unless you regard human genitals as a sort of cancerous affliction, a disease, a deformity, that came upon us after sin, then you cannot regard them as something that will be missing from our bodies after resurrection—any more than you can hold that Jesus' resurrected body was a eunuch's body. Here again, take the organs as emblem of deeper powers. The erotic powers with which we were created were given not only for this world, hence not only for reproduction. They were given as instruments and enactments of intimate union. That union culminates in union with God.

This might seem a rather pious conclusion to a scandalous meditation. Love of God is also not a cause for shame. Nor is the love of Jesus, as completely embodied. But then I want to insist that we come to the piety only after what seems a scandalous meditation on Jesus as erotic. Indeed, I want to argue more generally that we come to tell loving truths about Jesus only after we have forced ourselves to tell truths about our loves. At the decisive moment of this meditation, Jesus doesn't want you to enlist for his side because you are infatuated with his nobility. He wants you to look at your body with newly loving eyes because you have seen him as humanly beautiful even without nobility.

At the end of our meditation, we can reverse the familiar pronouncement that Christian *agape* defeats, excludes, or totally redoes "pagan" *eros*. The meditation teaches that there is no way into a full language of *agape* except through the language of *eros*. Meditating on our multiple shames before a sexed savior may help us a little out of shame, into salvation, which is wholeness. Meditating on Jesus' beauty even when crucified may help us a little toward a less fetishistic notion of beauty and its *eros*. Certainly, meditating on how we speak of our desire for Jesus shows us something about how to talk of his desires for us. Truth telling about *eros* comes before—and remains with—truth telling about *agape*. No other place to start Christian truth telling than face-to-face with Jesus.

CHRISTIAN W✪RDS

I N THE PRECEDING CHAPTERS, you have considered forms for suppressing, discovering, and offering truths in the Christian churches. The truths have been about sex, but therefore also about bureaucratic power, love, God, and incarnation. The chapters have been about truths, but mainly about efforts at truth telling. You have been asked to consider at many points what forms Christian speech might have for telling truths. Indeed, each of the central chapters has imitated an old form of Christian speech: the Scholastic sermon, the disputed question, the call to prayer, and the meditation on Christ. My choice to recall the forms has foreshadowed this last chapter, in which we consider, dear reader, what you and I have been doing together.

Let me propose that we have been doing two things. First, we have been correcting a terrible forgetfulness in Christian theology about how different kinds of truth require diverse language shapes. Second, we have been enacting the circuit of truth telling, which is always telling truths about something to someone. You are the someone—or may be.

Shapes for Truth

A S A RELIGION of conversion, Christianity has been a religion of persuasion. The earliest churches under-

stood themselves to be spreading by proclamation and witness, by preaching and showing the power of God newly dis-
played for the world. So, the early shapes for telling Christian
truth are shapes of persuasion. The canonical Gospels recall
teaching backed up by mighty deeds, but their purpose is not
simple recollection. Each narrative is a challenge to respond,
by conversion or endurance. So more obviously with the
canonical letters. They use a remarkable range of rhetorical
devices—some borrowed from Jewish or pagan models, some
improvised—to retrace paths of conversion and to propose
or impose good behavior. Even the Apocalypse of John, whatever else it is, is a rhetorically charged expression of faithful
longing that means both to elaborate and to confirm it.

Christian "theology," as we tend to reconstruct it, begins
with a more literary or school-like library of shapes for telling
its truths. To my ear, the early library is still self-consciously
persuasive. We are reminded in it how important rhetorical
training was in the late ancient world—reminded that someone like Augustine was by occupation a rhetorician and not
the leader of a philosophic school. So on for the rest of the library through the high Middle Ages and even into the early
modern period. We contemporary Christians inherit a rich
library of rhetorical shapes, not only in homilies or recorded
instructions, but in most of the major forms for Christian
writing. Why is it then that so much of modern theology is
unrhetorical or antirhetorical? Why is it that so much theology is now badly written in ways that make it unpersuasive?

You can take this question in several different directions.
It might lead, for example, to a study of the terms on which
theology first entered (Christian) universities and then of
how those terms changed as universities redefined themselves. Theology's loss of voice is partly the result of its being domesticated by contemporary universities, religious and

"secular." You might take the question, again, into the tangle
of confusion over what it means to become a multireligious
society, one in which various religions are supposed to be
equal before the law. Christian theologies have to find new
shapes, new voices, that no longer presume that Christianity
is or will be the dominant religion. Let me suggest that we
take the question in a third direction. We will use it to imagine what it would be to revivify some old Christian shapes for
truth telling.

Language wears down. In contemporary "Christendom,"
in the societies of mass media partly constructed by Christians, Christian language wears down fast. Finding new languages for Gospel truths might mean any number of things.
It might mean making new vocabularies, contriving new images, experimenting with new shapes. These acts of creation
take talent and time, both of which our churches now lack
more than they once did. So, finding fresh language must also
mean, in our present circumstances, the selective and critical
use of old forms of Christian speech. The use has got to be
selective. Not all of the old forms are worth reconsidering.
The use has also got to be critical. Many if not most of the
old forms have been badly misused. To bring them back into
play will require restoration, but also correction, adaptation,
improvisation.

I have tried to do just that in the middle chapters of this
book. How far I have succeeded, you should judge. Even if
you find my attempts to adapt particular forms unconvincing,
you ought to take the main lesson to heart: particular forms
are required for particular truths. No form could capture all
the truth about God—if it all could be captured in our languages. When you begin to believe that language can capture
truths completely, you turn from persuasion to recording, to
information storage. If you want to understand what Chris-

tian language has been and might be, if you want to see it as deeply persuasive, you would do much better to attend to the inadequacies of language, to the limits on its capacity to tell, describe, express. Persuasion is varied and repeatable. It needs to be done and redone. It ends each time by asking you to do something more, to go through the door of conviction or action opened for you. So, Christian persuasion supposes that church languages do not capture truth so much as foster right desire for it, which is not capturing truth but striving after it. The power in Christian language to move, to exhort, to proclaim is just the opposite of the arrogant notion that language is a container for complete truth. The power comes from language's frank admission that it cannot contain the truth. Language has power to move hearers toward truth.

Persuasive language can often be a lie. Who knows this better than we do? We live inside this extraordinary lying machine called mass advertising. Glib hawkers greet us at every turn—when we drive, pick up the telephone, read a magazine, click on a website, open our e-mail box, or pick up a branded bar of soap in the shower. Much of our fatigue with any claim for truth comes from our being constantly lied to most insultingly. We know as well that religious history is a history of conflicting persuasions. There are wolves in sheep's clothing. There are corrupters of speech in high church offices. We are shocked when we are told which words pedophile priests used to coerce boys into sex. We should also be shocked, and perhaps to just the same degree, by the corrosive lies that come in official documents or press conferences or even cathedral homilies. So, of course there are lies offered us as persuasions. Indeed, lying would seem to require a special effort at persuasion.

How might Christian communities resist the power of lying? They can never insure that lying won't happen because the capacity to tell truth is inseparable from power to lie. Indeed, the more powerful the truth you are telling, the more you activate the possibility of serious lying. Systems of tyrannical power are attracted to the power in truth telling in the way assassins are attracted to concealed weapons. The power to tell persuasive truths is attractive because it can be turned into the power to tell persuasive lies. This is clearest to me in texts about morals. You cannot write a persuasive moral text without giving grounds for violent misappropriation, because in attempting to reform character or community you necessarily energize the sources for character building and community formation. Once you show that certain means of persuasion work to build community, you tip off the tyrant's police: the same means might work to build an authoritarian community, a community of lies, a system of abusive power. The more persuasively you write Christian theology, the more you invite the police.

There is no way to insure against lying while telling the truth. You can only hope to recognize lies and disrupt them as they begin to insinuate themselves. How to do this in the shapes of Christian speech? One hopeful strategy for countering lying is to create persuasions that are self-disrupting by being constructively self-critical or gently self-mocking. Another is to make persuasion a respectful proposal rather than a threatening imposition. Yet another is to include multiple voices in every persuasion, to illustrate the importance of multiplicity, and to encourage the act of deliberate choice. Still, you should never believe that such strategies will remove the danger—the temptation—to lie. You cannot have liturgy or preaching without the threat of lying. You certainly cannot have theology without the constant temptation to lie. Christian speech always remains vulnerable. Each time we speak or write, we run a terrifying risk. It is a risk that we are called to take.

The call comes not least from an incarnate God. God in

flesh is vulnerable to lying, that is, to misrepresentation, false accusation, state torture, and execution. God in flesh does not try to forestall the violence of the lies. Jesus' vulnerability becomes another speaking of his truth. It is not only the thunderclap of resurrection that exposes the lie. It is exposed as well by the patience of truth under lying. I realize that this kind of reasoning can be put in service of some of the most tyrannical discourses of authoritarian churches. "We are the one, true church, and we remain confident in the proclamation of our truths especially when the world rages against us." A profession like that often means: "We have set ourselves up as a power on analogy to the world, and we expect you believers to be even more obedient to us than you would be to secular powers." But it is an indication of what I am saying that the truth about truth has so often been used to justify lies.

We keep on trying to speak truths in ever vulnerable words because we profess that God took flesh. Christian words imitate the incarnation. They are much-simplified icons of the incarnation. You know this, of course, and perhaps by heart, from the prologue of John's Gospel, with its hymn to the Word in so many senses. The Word takes flesh, and so there is a Gospel. The Word takes flesh, and so you are carefully confident that you can write a human hymn to a truth that is not undone by lies. You may even begin to believe that you are called to trust in the name of that flesh, "in his name" (1:12), as a way out of lies. God in flesh who speaks our language and bears one of our names—that God gives cautious, improbable confidence in speaking truth. The Word as the ground of our words: Augustine develops the notion of signification and incarnation in specifically rhetorical contexts, when talking about preparation and possibility for Christian preaching. Many other Christian writers follow him, using the incarnation as the occasion to reflect on their own speaking.

What can we do as Christian speakers to make our language more evidently incarnational? We can profess its vulnerability with confidence. The confidence doesn't point us toward a perfect language, toward invulnerable shapes for truth telling. It points us toward the flesh from which words come and the flesh toward which they go.

Listeners for Truth

T ELLING TRUTH in churches often feels like shouting into a lightless, echoless cavern. Or else like shouting into a thunderstorm. But truth isn't told to caves and storms (though it may come through them). It is told to people. Truth telling needs someone to listen. It needs a community that has fostered the conditions for truth telling. We can call this, if you like, a community of *agape*, but then we must immediately explain what we mean by that precious and endlessly abused word. *Agape* is both the effect and the precondition for telling truth. Truth proclaimed builds up the community of believers who are enjoined to love one another. One sign that they do love is that they can tell truths to one another—which means that they can hear truths from one another. We might then understand that here *agape* includes the committed respect and trust, the mutual gifts of attention and encouragement, that are required for full telling of truth. The community of *agape* is a community that hears truths about itself as something other than scandal. Since we can only talk about *agape* by talking through *eros*, we might say, more succinctly: the church must be a community with *eros* for truth. It must be an erotic community.[1]

The truths of this erotic community are not primarily propositions or assertions. They are carried in lives, liturgies, and ritual persuasions. The truths are shown in lives, because the divine truth is first of all for lives. These lives are instructed, expressed, and strengthened by sacraments in liturgy. They come close to propositions in preaching or professing creeds, but even then they are still understood as acts of community ritual. A creed is a profession, and preaching is a persuasion. So, propositional truth remains too narrow and weak a measure for the central acts of Christian truth telling. The truths in holy lives show only through chiaroscuro; they are shaded and shifting. The truths of liturgy can be gestures, "sacrifices," praises, or supplications. The best preachers' truths are often fictions, that is, artful constructions that entice us. We cannot measure this community's truth telling by some code of propositions.

How does the community for truth telling protect itself as a community against lying? We can fantasize a Christian community designed in such a way that it could not become falsely tyrannical, but such dreams end usually in very real tyrannies. What the community can do for protection is, in one sense, rather limited. It is also urgent. The community should be particularly careful how it attributes authority to its most valuable languages. As a listening and speaking community, it must attend to these languages' persuasive power in order to complicate it and disrupt it, to marvel at it and to undo it. Teaching must be practiced not as establishing regulations but as insisting on attention. So, obedience will mean not that you take as true whatever you are told, but that you commit yourself to consider carefully what is said to you. God, whose power is infinite, does not take flesh in order to terrify us into coerced submission. Christian communities should hardly use their (now even more paltry) authority to shout or sneer the language of coercion. The demand for unconditional assent to the pronouncements of any church officer violates the essential conditions for Christianity as a community of truth telling. An abuse of teaching authority undermines its own foundations.

Beyond taking great care for how it practices speaking and listening, a community for truth telling must seek to expect and to foster change. Truths are told to produce change— conversion, rededication, renewed ministry. These changes will lead—should lead, must lead—to changed tellings of truth. A community for Christian truth telling is a community that neither blocks nor manipulates changes in truthful speech. On the contrary, we might take "church" as a name for the community in which God continually enables true speech that is truly new. Powerful language is always vulnerable to the abuses of power. A community that looks to resist abuse is a community always looking to invert the relations of power present in language. It is a community that daily outwits the tyrannical possibilities of persuasion—precisely so that it can continue practicing persuasion.

Concluding Epistle

YOU WILL HAVE recognized that this concluding section is written in the form of an epistle. It is not pretending to be a bit of Scripture, of course. Indeed, this epistle claims no authority. It is written out of the conviction that there are readers—perhaps you are one of them—for whom the exchange of candid letters about scandal and honesty in churches is a way of building up churches. It is written out of the conviction that words can incarnate truth and that sharing truths makes church.

If I were to describe the epistle in less churchy language, I would call it a love letter. It is the kind of letter you write early in love, when you don't quite want to say that you are in love, because you are not at all sure which answer you'll hear back. So, it is filled with attempts at charm, with occasional disclosures, and with a lot of talk about how wonderful love can be—as if for other people. Still it is a love letter, and so it points toward an exchange of letters, to hoped-for volumes of future correspondence. It even hopes to become someday the kind of love letter in which the simplest recitation of household events becomes the fiercest declaration of passion. Only this love letter is not from one partner to another, not from one to another in a relation of two. This is a first, tentative love letter in the shambles of a community. It hopes to find enough community for correspondence.

We must have confidence, you and you and I, that the divine incitements to tell truth remain. We are in a sad and bitter scandal, and yet we are trying to exchange helpful words. We are in the ongoing and inevitable scandal that is any institutionalized church, and yet we ardently hope for another. Our confidence in Christian speech can be abused. So can our mutual commitment of attention. Perhaps I have abused yours in ways I didn't recognize. Perhaps you have abused mine in one minute or another. Still we attend. Still we act as if truths could be told even in churches—or especially in church.

NOTES

ONE / TELLING TRUTHS IN A "CHURCH CRISIS"

1. In the paragraphs following, I summarize newspaper stories published almost daily in the *Dallas Morning News* from the beginning of May to the end of July 1997, chiefly from reporting by Ed Housewright, Brooks Egerton, and Peter Slover.

2. On April 23, 2002, the Associated Press quoted Gregory as saying, "It is an ongoing struggle to make sure that the Catholic priesthood is not dominated by homosexual men." On the same date, CNN carried a very similar quotation: "It is most importantly a struggle to make sure that the Catholic priesthood is not dominated by homosexual men."

3. *Newsweek*, May 6, 2002, pp. 26–28.

4. For example, John Paul II, *Sacramentorum sanctitatis tutela* [Apostolic Letter on Crimes Reserved to the Congregation for the Doctrine of the Faith, April 30, 2001], *Acta Apostolicae Sedis* 113 (2001): 737–739, with the procedural regulations in the Congregation's *Epistula de delictis gravioribus eidem Congregationi pro Doctrinae fidei reservatis* [May 18, 2001], *Acta Apostolicae Sedis* 113 (2001): 785–788.

5. Norman Rockwell, "Freedom of Speech/Buy War Bonds" (1943).

6. For those who feel compelled to locate this book on the map of contemporary academic theology, I can provide a few coordinate points. First, the book accepts both the claim that holiness requires abiding in unpopular truth (Hauerwas) and the warning that Christian churches have exhausted themselves trying to manage truths for power (Foucault). Then, second, the book moves forward between the (apocalyptic) hope that churches will reverberate with a symphony of truthful voices (von Balthasar) and the insistence that the voices most in need of doubling are the voices of freeing, searing testimony (Chopp). Finally, third, the book takes seriously recent efforts to relocate religious speech in a social world that is little more than a mass market for "ideas" and images (Milbank, but then Ward, but then again Vattimo). The texts in question (and in order) are Stanley Hauerwas, *Sanctify Them in the Truth: Holiness Exemplified* (Nashville: Abingdon Press, 1998), with particular attention to the curious comment on Foucault at p. 61, note 1; Michel Foucault, "Christianity and Confession," in *The Politics of Truth*, ed. Sylvère Lotringer and Lysa Hochroth (New York: Semiotext[e], 1997), 199–235, read into the context of Foucault's last lectures on truth telling, de-

scribed, for example, in Thomas Flynn, "Foucault as Parrhesiast: His Last Course at the Collège de France (1984)," in *The Final Foucault*, ed. James Bernauer and David Rasmussen (Cambridge, Mass.: MIT Press, 1988), 102–118; Hans Urs von Balthasar, *Truth Is Symphonic: Aspects of Christian Pluralism*, trans. Graham Harrison (San Francisco: Ignatius Press, 1987), especially 86–87; Rebecca Chopp, "Reimagining Public Discourse," *Journal of Theology for Southern Africa*, no. 103 (March 1999): 33–48, especially 38–44, and earlier in *The Power to Speak: Feminism, Language, God* (New York: Crossroad, 1989), especially 59–62 and 66–70; John Milbank perhaps most succinctly in "Knowledge: Theological Critique of Philosophy in Hamann and Jacobi," in *Radical Orthodoxy: A New Theology*, ed. Milbank, Catherine Pickstock, and Graham Ward (London: Routledge, 1999), 21–37; Graham Ward, *Cities of God* (London: Routledge, 2000), especially 52–77; Gianni Vattimo, *Belief*, trans. Luca D'Isanto and David Webb (Stanford, Calif.: Stanford University Press, 1999), especially 38–43. Listing these titles together, I see that the map may not be of contemporary theology so much as of the top of my desk.

7. I have kept away from cumbersome scholarly apparatus. I know that there are hundreds of important books pertinent to what I say. I know, too, that any one of the topics I treat here has been and will be the occasion or excuse for hundreds of volumes more. This little book is a collection of revised lectures, and so it is not an appropriate occasion for brandishing my scholarly credentials or displaying how much I can cite—if there ever is an appropriate occasion for such vanities.

TWO / TELLING SECRETS: SCANDAL AND CHURCH REFORM

1. Sometimes I am asked, with surprise or indignation, "Are you still a Catholic?" I usually reply, "Tell me which of the dozens of definitions of 'Catholic' you have in mind and I'll do my best to answer." You will see soon enough that I myself do not define Catholicism as verbal submission to the latest decrees from the Vatican. I do not define it that way because of my understanding of the divine gift of faith, but also because of my understanding of tradition. To have a tradition is precisely not to be subject to a single authority in the present. So, I think of myself as a Talmudic Catholic: I choose to inherit Catholic traditions, which means that I have the responsibility to think through them about their contradictions and to wonder with them about who gets to count as part of the tradition.

2. The epistle reads, "But whorish copulation (*porneia*) and all uncleanness (*akatharsia*), or greed, are not even to be named among you, as befits the holy." The two Greek words in parentheses are hard to understand, because their meanings are changeable and too comprehensive. The vagueness in the terms has encouraged odd misreadings. In the older traditions, *porneia* and greed were set aside and *akatharsia* was arbitrarily specified as same-sex genital activity. So, the homoerotic acts became instances of the "nameless sin."

3. I consider the rhetorical force of this charge and some of its historical examples in *The Invention of Sodomy in Christian Theology* (Chicago: University of Chicago Press, 1997), 48–51, 101–102, 133–135, and *The Silence of Sodom: Homosexuality in Modern Catholicism* (Chicago: University of Chicago Press, 2000), 113–139.

4. For example, Foucault, "Christianity and Confession," 202.

5. James Alison has said this in many places, but with particular force in *Faith Beyond Resentment: Fragments Catholic and Gay* (London: Darton, Longman, and Todd, 2001), perhaps especially ix–xiii.

6. If the choice seems too severe, you might want to go to my longer form of the argument in *Silence of Sodom*, 21–82. There, I try to show from contemporary and historical examples the ways in which official theological speech has been composed to prevent the possibility of counterargument.

7. Jordan, *Silence of Sodom*, 141–208.

8. Unsigned review of *Silence of Sodom*, *Publishers Weekly*, April 24, 2000.

9. "Father Guido Sarducci" was a chain-smoking, cassock-wearing monologuist created by Don Novello in the early 1970s. After appearing on *Chicken Little Comedy Hour* and the Smothers Brothers' 1975 return, "Father" went on to his greatest fame as a regular on *Saturday Night Live*. See Doug Hill and Jeff Weingrad, *Saturday Night: A Backstage History of Saturday Night Life* (New York: Beech Tree Books/William Morrow, 1986), 287.

10. Romano Guardini, "The Church and the Catholic," in *The Church and the Catholic, and the Spirit of the Liturgy*, trans. Ada Lane (New York: Sheed & Ward, 1935), 55: "Christ lives on in the Church, but Christ Crucified. One might almost venture to suggest that the defects of the Church are His Cross. The entire Being of the mystical Christ—His truth, His holiness, His grace, and His adorable person—are nailed to them, as once His physical Body to the wood of the Cross. And he who will have Christ, must take His Cross as well. We cannot separate Him from it." Dorothy Day paraphrases Guardini's remark more boldly in *The Long Loneliness* (San Francisco: Harper San Francisco, 1997), 150: "Romano Guardini said the Church is the Cross on which Christ was crucified; one could not separate Christ from His Cross, and one must live in a state of permanent dissatisfaction with the Church" (to which compare p. 218).

11. Beverly Wildung Harrison, "The Power of Anger in the Work of Love: Christian Ethics for Women and Other Strangers," in *Making the Connections: Essays in Feminist Social Ethics*, ed. Carol Robb (Boston: Beacon Press, 1985), 3–21.

12. Wayne Koestenbaum, *The Queen's Throat: Opera, Homosexuality, and the Mystery of Desire* (New York: Random House, Vintage Books, 1994), 39, 113, respectively.

13. See Jordan, *Silence of Sodom*, 92–93, for the case and the citations.

14. For Farinata, Dante, *Inferno* 10.

15. Simone Weil, "La personne et le sacré: Collectivité—personne—impersonnel—droit—justice," in Weil, *Écrits de Londres et dernières lettres* (Paris: Gallimard, 1957), 11–44, at 14.

16. Weil, "La personne et le sacré," 28–29.

17. For Bernardino's preaching on sodomy, see Michael Rocke, *Forbidden Friendships: Homosexuality and Male Culture in Renaissance Florence* (New York: Oxford University Press, 1996), 36–44; and, much more extensively, Franco Mormando, *The Preacher's Demons: Bernardino of Siena and the Social Underworld of Early Renaissance Italy* (Chicago: University of Chicago Press, 1999), 109–163.

18. In what follows, I translate from Bernadino of Siena, *De horrendo peccato contra naturam*, in his *Opera omnia*, ed. the Fathers of the Collegium S. Bonaventurae, vol. 3 (Quaracchi: Collegium S. Bonaventurae, 1966), 267–284. The *themata* for the three articles are taken from Ps. 57:4–6; the hortatory *prothema* is John 5:8, which is the day's reading from the Gospel.

19. For a collection of passages, see Mormando, *Preacher's Demons*, 148–150.

THREE / TELLING LOVES: SAME-SEX UNIONS AND CHATTER ABOUT MARRIAGE

1. I feel that I ought to apologize for the awkward phrase "icon loop." The best apology may be a brief explanation. By "icon loop," I mean to recall not just that the icons are repetitive, but that they blend picture and sound and that they are shown for money (as the loops in a porno arcade). I also want to recall the way "sound looping" in movie production supplies clear voices after the filming—it scripts those voices better. I am using *icon* quite deliberately, because I mean to recall at once the profound theology of holy icons in Eastern Christian churches and the now familiar use of the term for descriptions of mass culture. For the force of "mechanical," see Walter Benjamin, "The Work of Art in the Age of Mechanical Reproduction," in *Illuminations*, ed. Hannah Arendt (New York: Schocken Books, 1969), 217–251.

2. *Chatter* may seem harsh. It is in fact an allusion to an English translation of a harsh remark by Kierkegaard's pseudonym, Johannes Climacus: "In all human probability the centuries-old echo, like the echo in some of our churches, would not only have riddled faith with chatter but would have eliminated it in chatter." See Søren Kierkegaard, *Philosophical Fragments*, ed. and trans. Howard V. Hong and Edna H. Hong (Princeton, N.J.: Princeton University Press, 1985), 71.

3. The historical argument here is one I try to make more fully in *Ethics of*

Sex (Oxford: Basil Blackwell, 2002), 47–75, where I also supply citations to exemplary texts.

4. Alison Lurie, *Familiar Spirits: A Memoir of James Merrill and David Jackson* (New York: Viking Penguin, 2001), 38–39.

5. I am tempted to call this the "Myra/Myron" strategy in honor of Gore Vidal's hero(ine), who manages to escape not only from cruelly opposed gender scripts, but from an endless and englobing replay of *Siren of Babylon* (1949). See Vidal, *Myron* (New York: Random House, 1974).

6. I am proposing a general reform of Christian speech and not a two-tier system in churches where there would be other-sex "marriages" and same-sex "unions." Christians should give over the word *marriage* to the state, the advertisers, and their churchly allies. They should use *unions* for all erotic relationships blessed by Christian communities.

7. The nearly canonical text in this regard is now Judith Butler, *Gender Trouble: Feminism and the Subversion of Identity* (New York: Routledge, 1990); but it is worth remembering such earlier and delightfully concrete analyses of gender performances as Erving Goffman, *Gender Advertisements* (New York: Colophon Books/Harper and Row, 1979).

8. The complications of gender role in mystical writing—and in writings about mysticism—are beautifully traced in Jeffrey J. Kripal, *Roads of Excess, Palaces of Wisdom: Eroticism and Reflexivity in the Study of Mysticism* (Chicago: University of Chicago Press, 2001).

9. I have in mind Roland Barthes, *A Lover's Discourse*, trans. Richard Howard (New York: Hill and Wang, 1978); and Julia Kristeva, *Tales of Love*, trans. Leon S. Roudiez (New York: Columbia University Press, 1987), not least in the extraordinary "Stabat Mater," 234–263.

10. This is the marvelous test proposed by Gayatri Chakravorty Spivak, "The Politics of Translation," in *Outside in the Teaching Machine* (New York: Routledge, 1993), 179–200, at 187: "To decide whether you are prepared enough to start translating, then, it might help if you have graduated into speaking, by choice or preference, of intimate matters in the language of the original." We ought to make that a rule for moral theologians—and not only when they translate.

11. Mark Doty, "Letter to Walt Whitman," in *Source* (New York: Harper-Collins, 2002), 24–33, at 30.

FOUR / TELLING GOD: HONESTY IN THEOLOGY

1. In Acts 17:34 someone called "Dionysius the Areopagite" becomes a believer and joins Paul after Paul's generally unsuccessful preaching in the Areopagus.

2. I use the order deliberately adopted for the complete English translation

by Paul Rorem and defended by him elsewhere. *Pseudo-Dionysius: The Complete Works*, trans. Colm Luibhead and Paul Rorem (New York: Paulist Press, 1987); and Paul Rorem, *Pseudo-Dionysius: A Commentary on the Texts and an Introduction to Their Influence* (New York: Oxford University Press, 1993), especially 206–210. You can infer the order most quickly by connecting the backward map of the corpus and announced plans in *Mystical Theology* 3 with the back reference in *Celestial Hierarchy* 15:6 and the absence of forward references to the other works in *Celestial Hierarchy* or *Ecclesiastical Hierarchy*. There are further complications here, including the question of the traditional orders for the treatises, but the cross-references will give us enough for a beginning.

3. Important twentieth-century schools of Protestant theology were indeed traditions of "negative moral theology." We ought to feel it as a sharp loss that they now seem distant.

4. Ps-Dionysius, *Divine Names*, 4:11–12, as in *Complete Works*, 80–81; compare *Celestial Hierarchy* 2:4 (*Complete Works*, 150). In both passages, the English "yearning" translates *eros;* in the second, "desire" translates *epithumia*.

5. Perfect and painful examples can be found in the unthinking use of categories like "pedophile" or "ephebophile" in church discourses. However useful these terms may be in certain clinical contexts, they cannot simply be drafted into churchly use.

6. This is the main argument of Michel Foucault, *History of Sexuality*, vol. 1: *An Introduction*, trans. Robert Hurley (New York: Vintage Books/Random House, 1980). Foucault's ironic and rhetorically clever text has led to extraordinary misunderstandings. These are diagnosed and corrected in two recent essays by David Halperin, "Forgetting Foucault: Acts, Identities, and the History of Sexuality," *Representations* 63 (1998): 93–120, and "How to Do the History of Male Homosexuality," *GLQ: A Journal of Lesbian and Gay Studies* 6 (2000): 87–123.

7. See Jonathan Ned Katz, *The Invention of Heterosexuality* (New York: Dutton Signet/Penguin, 1995), especially 83–97.

8. There are now many attempts to speak the importance of the erotic to Christian life, but one of the most powerfully and soberly hopeful remains Carter Heyward, *Touching Our Strength: The Erotic as Power and the Love of God* (San Francisco: Harper and Row, 1989).

9. Here, I am thinking not only of Vattimo's argument in *Belief*, but of the ironic conclusion to an essay by Adorno: "I see no other possibility than an extreme ascesis towards any type of revealed faith, an extreme loyalty to the prohibition of images, far beyond what this once originally meant." See his "Reason and Revelation," in *Critical Models: Interventions and Catchwords*, trans. Henry W. Pickford (New York: Columbia University Press, 1998), 135–142, at 142.

FIVE / TELLING GOD'S BODY: THE FLESH OF INCARNATION

1. The series *Son of God* premiered on BBC One April 1, 2001. The image was released to the press on March 27 of that year.

2. There are also silences about the body of Jesus in the current quest for its historical truth. John Dominic Crossan's marvelous chapter title "In the Beginning Is the Body" covers a text chiefly healing miracles and patronage. Certainly, it doesn't begin with *Jesus'* body. See Crossan, *Jesus: A Revolutionary Biography* (San Francisco: Harper San Francisco, 1995), 75–101. Geza Vermes, in his much longer *The Changing Faces of Jesus* (New York: Penguin Compass, 2000), not only avoids the physical face, but deals with other aspects of Jesus' bodily life either by dismissing them as fabulous or by treating them as lived scriptural citations. Jesus' circumcision is another "amusing snippet of a semilegendary nature" (229) and his celibacy refers to interpretations of what is required for prophetic life, as exemplified by Philo on Moses (273). History, too, can hide the body—or ignore it because of uncertain evidence.

3. We are beginning to get some provocative theological writing on Jesus' body as a sexed body, though much of it is discounted as "feminist" or "queer" theology. See, for example, Robert Goss, *Jesus Acted Up: A Gay and Lesbian Manifesto* (San Francisco: Harper San Francisco, 1992), especially 69–72 and 81–85; and Carter Heyward, *Saving Jesus from Those Who Are Right: Rethinking What It Means to Be Christian* (Minneapolis: Fortress Press, 1999), 123–127.

4. Ignatius of Loyola, *Spiritual Exercises*, Second Week, perhaps especially paragraphs [92]–[98] and [143]–[146], as in his *Obras completas*, ed. Ignacio Iparraguirre (Madrid: Biblioteca de Autores Cristianos, 1963), 218–220, 226–227.

5. See Leo Steinberg's justly famous *The Sexuality of Christ in Renaissance Art and in Modern Oblivion*, 2d ed. (Chicago: University of Chicago Press, 1995). Steinberg is himself nervous that his topic will seem scandalous (e.g., pp. 24, 36, 41).

6. See the examples in Richard C. Trexler, "Gendering Jesus Crucified," in *Iconography at the Crossroads*, ed. Brendan Cassidy (Princeton, N.J.: Index of Christian Art, Department of Art and Archaeology, Princeton University, 1993), 107–119, at 113–115; and Javier Perez Escohotado, *Sexo e Inquisición en España* (Madrid: Temas de Hoy, 1992), 211–214, 219.

7. I keep speaking of Catholic art because I have lived in it. I suspect that the same is true for other Christian traditions only with significant qualifications. The Eastern churches are constrained both by their iconoclastic prohibitions on statuary and by different iconographic emphases. Protestant traditions have long regarded Catholic art—and perhaps especially Catholic representations of Jesus' body—as idolatrous or morbid.

8. There is an old spiritual precept, "Follow the naked Christ naked." It has many allegorical and liturgical applications (e.g., in baptismal rites), but it has also been applied more literally in ascetical and penitential practices. For the desert monks, both demons and great saints arrive in the nude.

9. In this way, too, Christians might reply to one of Nietzsche's most pointed criticisms; namely, that any true god would appear as naked because unashamed. "But such a god [as Dionysus] has nothing to do with all this venerable lumber and pomp. 'Keep that,' he would say, 'for yourself and your like and for anyone else who needs it! I—have no reason to cover my naked-ness.'" See Friedrich Nietzsche *Beyond Good and Evil*, no. 295, trans. R. J. Hollingdale (New York: Viking Penguin, 1973), 201.

10. There are tantalizing bits of evidence outside the canonical Gospels, es-pecially in "Gnostic" gospels or other texts that emphasize secret initiation by Christ. But it is perhaps more interesting to recall that speculation about Jesus' "orientation" did not begin with Stonewall. It runs in English litera-ture back beyond the first appearances of the word *homosexuality*.

11. Compare Thomas Aquinas, *Summa theologiae* part 3 question 15 article 2: "And in this way, the flesh of Christ, by the desire of the sensitive appetite, naturally had appetite for food and drink and sleep, and other things for which there can be appetite according to right reason." The roundabout phrasing shows the problem about attributing anything like our sexual de-sires to Christ. Christ would have had sexual "appetite" only according to right reason, that is, for the sake of procreation in a monogamous and per-manent union of a man and a woman. If he had copulated in such a union, he would have indeed felt sexual pleasure (compare *Summa* part 1 question 98 article 2 reply to objection 3, on hypothetical sexual pleasure in Eden). Since Jesus was not married, it would have been irrational for him to suffer sexual desires. Thomas is not at all hesitant to affirm that Jesus had genitals. He argues elsewhere in the *Summa* that it was appropriate for the Lord to be circumcised partly in order to show "the truth of his human flesh" (*Summa* 3:37.1).

12. John Paul II, *Ordinatio sacerdotalis* [Apostolic Letter on Reserving Priestly Ordination to Men Alone, May 22, 1994], together with Congre-gation for the Doctrine of the Faith, *Responsum ad dubium* [Concerning the Teaching Contained in *Ordinatio sacerdotalis*, October 28, 1995], and the ac-companying, clarifying letter from Joseph Ratzinger on the same date.

13. Barton's impulses are recounted and analyzed in Stephen Moore's *God's Beauty Parlor and Other Queer Spaces in and around the Bible* (Stanford Uni-versity Press, 2001), 105–107.

14. Worry over the effeminacy of Christ in Protestant portraiture has yielded much to recent study. See, for example, Colleen McDannell, *Material Chris-tianity: Religion and Popular Culture in America* (New Haven, Conn.: Yale University Press, 1995), 180–181; David Morgan, *Visual Piety: A History and*

Theory of Popular Religious Images (Berkeley: University of California Press, 1998), 111–123; and Moore, *God's Beauty Parlor*, 107–117.

15. Robert Neville shows how our (erotic) views on Jesus viewing us can be taken up into the larger language of friendship. See Neville, *Symbols of Jesus: A Christology of Symbolic Engagement* (Cambridge, England: Cambridge University Press, 2001), 199–223, especially 214–217.

16. The tradition is introduced in Moore, *God's Beauty Parlor*, 96–99.

17. Bonaventure, *Itinerarium*, 7:6, in *The Journey of the Mind to God*, trans. Philotheus Boehner, ed. Stephen F. Brown (Indianapolis: Hackett, 1993), 39. Not coincidentally, the remark follows a quotation from Ps-Dionysius.

18. Julian of Norwich, *Showings*, trans. Edmund Colledge and James Walsh (Mahwah, N.J.: Paulist Press, 1978), 128 ("everything around the cross was ugly to me"), 129 (blood), 136–137 (blood), 141 ("his freshness, his ruddiness, his vitality and his beauty" which, with death, now changes), and so on.

19. My student was remembering the arguments in Anders Nygren, *Agape and Eros*, trans. Philip S. Watson (London: SPCK, 1957), as summarized, for example, in a chart on p. 210. Elsewhere in the book Nygren simply says that *eros* is the "principal adversary" of Christianity (53). My argument in this chapter is that Nygren must be wrong not least because his teaching would deny the incarnation.

20. For help with how to begin examining our supposed familiarity with this language, see again Kripal, *Roads of Excess*, perhaps beginning from pp. 15–23.

21. Rediscoveries sometimes happen at surprising sites, say, in Hans Urs von Balthasar. See Gerard Loughlin, "God's Sex," in *Radical Orthodoxy: A New Theology*, ed. John Milbank, Catherine Pickstock, and Graham Ward (London: Routledge, 1999), 143–162.

SIX / CHRISTIAN WORDS

1. Graham Ward uses this phrase to motivate and conclude an account of what churches might be as spaces around the Eucharistic Body. See Ward, *Cities of God*, 152–181. I use it in a homelier sense (which is only part of Ward's meaning). I mean that churches ought to be communities in which *eros* is protected and educated.

ACKNOWLEDGMENTS

There would be no book except for the invitation from the School of Theology at Boston University to deliver its Brown Lectures in March 2002. I am especially grateful to Robert Neville for inviting me, hosting me, instructing me, and befriending me.

An earlier version of chapter 2 was presented before a lively and helpful audience at the Pacific School of Religion. My thanks to them and to my hosts, Mary Ann Tolbert and Bernard Schlager.

I was able to write chapter 3 because of my participation in the work of Emory's Center for the Interdisciplinary Study of Religion. I am most grateful to John Witte, its director, and to the other Senior Fellows, who together formed a seminar remarkable for its energy and its lack of academic pretension.

Other friends have been generous enough to read the whole book in manuscript. My gratitude and my sympathies go to Dirk Lange, Alf McCartney, Joy McDougall, and Ted Smith. One of my oldest and wisest friends, Sally Dunn, sat with me in conversation through the final writing of the whole text. She reminded me of a phrase we both learned in the first week of freshman Greek: κοινὰ τὰ φίλων. The things of friends are in common. Their writing, too.

INDEX